CW00735206

Danielle Jackson is a certified holistic nutrition coach, yoga teacher, personal trainer and qualified school teacher from the UK. She is on a mission to inspire and transform as many people as she can to live a healthy, more vibrant, energised and beautiful life.

Danielle holds workshops on nutrition and yoga currently around Dubai and the UK with a goal to take this to further destinations around the world. She specialises in eating disorders, anti-aging, eating for beauty, gut health, weight loss, superfoods and healing your body from within.

After Danielle was diagnosed with an autoimmune disorder at the young age of 18, she set off on a mission to heal her body from within using only food. After extensive research over the past eighteen-plus years, Danielle is now ready to share everything she has learnt.

It is her absolute passion to inspire others to make a change to their current lifestyles and dietary choices so they can become more beautiful from within, STOP emotionally eating, slow down aging, achieve gorgeous, glowing skin, prevent or heal from chronic illnesses, and fully start to enjoy living in a healthy, beautiful and strong body.

As the quote goes...

"Most people have no idea how good their body is designed to feel."
It is Dani's mission to get you there.

This book is dedicated to ALL my readers.

I have written this book from my heart to help all of you beautiful people out there achieve ultimate health and radiance. I struggled for many years, trying to find the answers to my own health and beauty concerns and this is the reason why I wrote this book. I don't want you to struggle like I did; I want YOU to have ALL the answers at hand and use this book to free you from every misinformation you have read so you can truly become beautiful and healthy inside and out. I hope it inspires you to make a few positive changes to your lifestyle that will benefit ALL of your health and beauty needs. Love Dani x.

Danielle Jackson

BEAUTY AND THE GUT

AUSTIN MACAULEY PUBLISHERS™

LONDON • CAMBRIDGE • NEW YORK • SHARJAH

A CIP catalogue record for this title is available from the British Library.

ISBN 9781788781800 (Paperback)
ISBN 9781788781817 (Hardback)
ISBN 9781788781824 (E-Book)

www.austinmacauley.com

First Published (2018)
Austin Macauley Publishers Ltd™
25 Canada Square
Canary Wharf
London
E14 5LQ

I would like to extend so much gratitude to my parents, Ralph and Jean, for their unwavering support and love. Thank you for giving me wings to fly and for really believing in me. Without your support and love, I wouldn't have had the strength to continue to follow my heart and dreams. I love you both so much.

Thank you also to my supportive friends (you all know who you are) who have assisted me in this crazy journey I've been on through the last couple of years. Without your help, I wouldn't have made it and this book may never have been written. Big love to all of you, you couldn't see what my vision was and yet you still believed in me and helped me as much as you could. I am forever grateful to you all.

Thank you to everyone who crossed my path in the last couple of years. Each one of you has played a part in helping me to write this book. All of my clients, yoga teachers, personal trainers, teachers – you all inspired me along the way to keep writing.

I said I wanted an adventurous life and I got what I asked for. The last 2 years certainly have been.

Love to everyone who stood by me, even when you thought I was crazy for leaving a secure teaching job to leap into the unknown, without a home or a steady income, because I HAD to follow my heart's calling.

THANK YOU ALL. BIG LOVE
Dani xxx

Table of Contents

Chapter 1
Introduction

At the young age of 12, I remember my first pimple appearing, which later turned into a full blown acne. I was covered. My back, my neck, my chest, my shoulders and my face. No joke, it was everywhere. I felt gross. I covered my face with toxic make-up to try to conceal it and make myself feel prettier but it just made my skin worse. I then developed blackheads, whiteheads and enlarged pores. I didn't know what to do. I couldn't wear strappy tops that showed my shoulders or my back, as I looked horrific. Not only were they hideous to look at they also caused me a great deal of pain. They looked like boils. I spent a good few years trying to get rid of them with various off the shelf toxic cosmetics. I would bathe in Dettol baths, steam my face, go to saunas, sunbeds and try the newest acne lotion to dry out my skin. I even went to the doctors for medication. I was prescribed various antibiotics to take internally as well as apply externally onto the skin to kill the acne, nothing worked. I really didn't like myself much and was at a loss as to how to overcome my acne problem. I just wanted to feel as pretty as my friends and be able to show off my shoulders in nice little dresses but it seemed impossible. By the age of 15, I was still suffering. I had now lived with acne for over 3 years; surely I thought, this had to end soon? Later on, my doctor made me an appointment to see a dermatologist. She recommended that I take a pill called 'Roaccutane'. After some research I found that Roaccutane WILL clear up acne but it could also make you very sick, in fact one of the side effects is the possibility of infertility. I didn't feel this was the way forward for me.

By the age of 16, I was still suffering with acne. After another visit to the doctor he recommended that I go on 'the pill', which, as nothing else was working, I agreed to. (Note, not once did my doctor or dermatologist ask what my diet was like). My acne slowly began to clear up. YAY, finally after 4 years of suffering I could get to show off my shoulders. Unfortunately, only 3 years later I was then diagnosed with an autoimmune disorder (Graves' disease, a condition that attacks the thyroid gland). This came as a shock. Oh man! More doctors! I was just 18 years old, studying at university for my degree in 'Performance Arts'. One day a course friend said to me that my neck looked quite swollen. "Do you have a thyroid problem?" she asked. She had noticed my neck because she had a similar problem herself some time ago. She recommended that I call the doctor ASAP to get it checked out because it looked like I had a thyroid goitre. I had never even heard of a thyroid. What was that?

I immediately informed my mum and told her what had happened so she made an appointment to see the doctor. After blood tests were taken, they confirmed I had Graves' disease. I had never heard of this disease and the doctor had no concrete explanation as to how I had developed it, however, he did tell me that it can be brought on by stress, or if it runs in the family I could have inherited it. As there was no one in the family at that time, which had contracted this disease, it definitely wasn't hereditary.

I was prescribed beta blockers for my heart palpitations and carbimazole to lower the levels of thyroxine I was over producing. They didn't work. I was then informed the only option open to me now was to have my thyroid removed or destroyed, (again note; the doctor never once asked me what my diet was like). Left with no other choice, I underwent Radioactive Iodine Treatment to destroy my thyroid – for life! Prior to this treatment, I was unaware of the function of the thyroid gland; I had no idea at this time how important your thyroid is, all I knew was I just wanted to feel well again. I was suffering from depression and anxiety. I had chronic fatigue. I was binge-eating on everything bad for me. I went from a size 8 to a size 16 in around 6 months. I lost all my confidence. I had to take time off from my university studies for a year to recover and feel well again but was not sure how I would do that. How would I get back to a healthy, slim and energised me?

After years of continuous research, I have finally found the link between my acne and autoimmune disorder and this is what I would like to share with you in this book. It all comes down to one thing – HOW HEALTHY IS YOUR GUT? If your gut isn't healthy, you won't be healthy and neither will your skin. Looking back, if I had been aware of the role the gut plays on our health and beauty, I may never have developed Graves' disease and I could have healed my acne worries earlier.

The Thyroid

I'm not going to talk much about the thyroid but as I had mine destroyed by radioactive iodine treatment; I felt it appropriate to make a brief mention of the role the thyroid plays.

Little do we realise that the thyroid is a very important gland, which needs to function well in order to have a healthy body. I really wish I still had a functioning one. The thyroid gland produces a hormone called 'thyroxine'. If the thyroid is unable to efficiently produce and distribute thyroxine around the body, many disturbances in the body may occur. For example, irritability of the nerves, depression, damage to teeth and muscles, thickening and coarsening of the skin, dry hair, hair loss, wasting of body tissue, lethargy, weight gain, forgetfulness, loss of libido, anxiety, slow metabolism and these are just a few. This small gland has a BIG impact on our health and our beauty. The thyroid gland regulates our metabolic rate controlling the oxidation in cells and keeps the body functioning and regenerating itself. It is a VERY important gland. We need it!

Let's take a deeper look into BEAUTY AND THE GUT.

Your internal world is the first step to get you back to radiance and health.

Chapter 2
Skin

Skin is the mirror of our health. It tells us what is going on inside our bodies. It mirrors our emotional state, our hormones, toxins, nutrition, oxygen, water and essential fatty oils.

If your skin is dry, flaky, irritated, oily, spotty, itchy, is aging fast, has lost elasticity, has no glow. You are not healthy! Your gut is not healthy.

Nothing will show up on your skin unless there is seepage of toxins from the kidneys and liver. Placing lotions and potions onto your skin is not going to fix that spot, wrinkle or rash. You need to look within and see what is going on inside, and then the outside will start to clean up and will have you glowing, beautiful and healthy once again.

Our skin is affected by everything: our thoughts, moods, digestion, sleep, water, minerals, stress, hormones, chemicals, our environment etc., but it is predominately affected by what we eat/drink and our gut microbiome. If your skin is inflamed, it is because your gut is inflamed.

Skin is the body's largest elimination organ. When the liver and kidneys are overloaded with rubbish, they can't handle it. All the bad things then begin to circulate into our blood, leaving toxins to start seeping out through the pores of our skin.

Your skin is a reflection of your internal world. Beautiful, healthy skin needs to have clean pure blood. This all comes down to what you put into your mouth.

> **The secret to beautiful skin is in the intestines and the liver.**

All the lotions, potions and pills out there on the shelves today are full of toxic chemicals, which will not help your skin glow; heal acne, slow down aging, make your hair grow faster, help you lose weight or heal your body. You have to dig deeper. **Beauty and health come from within.**

Beauty begins in THE GUT!

Chapter 3
Love Your Gut

Have you ever suffered from a bad stomach ache? Have you ever had to run to the bathroom after you've eaten? Have you ever said, "No, I can't eat that; it doesn't agree with me?"

Do you get gas and bloating after you eat? Do you suffer with bad breath? Maybe you have diarrhoea/constipation or heartburn? Do you have eczema? Do you have psoriasis or acne? Do you ever suffer from brain fog? Do you have chronic fatigue? Are your joints inflamed? Do you feel lethargic? Do you have migraines? Do you have weight problems? If you answered yes to any of these, then YES – you may have a gut problem.

Research over the past 2 decades has revealed that gut health is critical to overall health, and that an unhealthy gut contributes to a wide range of diseases such as diabetes, obesity, autoimmune disorders, rheumatoid arthritis, depression, cancer, chronic fatigue syndrome and many other diseases that are NOT connected to digestion. Therefore, restoring your gut health is one of the keys to a happy, long, beautiful and healthy life.

> **Hippocrates** – (The father of natural medicine) states, "*All disease begins in the gut.*" Not 50% or 80% – **ALL DISEASE!**

Your gut is the hub of good health. We are frequently told you are what you eat but this isn't the case, '*you are what you can absorb*'.

Your gut is so important. This is where you absorb **ALL** of your food.

Did you know your gut contains around 70%-80% of your immune system? Yes, that's right! Your immune system is in your gut. So when you feel a cold coming on or have that run down feeling, always look to your gut first.

Your gut is also considered to be your second brain. A nerve called 'THE VAGUS NERVE' intertwines both the brain and gut. The gut is often considered to be the second brain because the gut and the brain are in constant communication. Many vital brain-communicating chemicals such as 'serotonin' are made in the gut and this is why having a healthy gut also leads to good mental health as well as physical health. Research has proven that diseases such as, autism, Alzheimer's and schizophrenia are all connected to the gut. So if you feel like your brain seems foggy, this implies that your gut is on fire so your brain dulls in response to your upset gut.

> **Believe it or not, our intestines are the key to how we look and feel.**

How Does Digestion Work?

Digestion begins in the mouth with chewing and ends in the small intestine. We need to be chewing our food properly. Our stomach doesn't have teeth, and when you don't chew your food well that half-digested food can also become toxic and foreign to the body. You need to try to chew your food until it is liquid. Ideally, you should be chewing your food at least 30 times before you swallow. This will really make a HUGE difference to your beauty and gut health. Try it!

Food then passes to the stomach and then through the GI tract where it mixes with digestive juices, causing large molecules of food to break down into smaller molecules. The body then absorbs these smaller molecules through the walls of the small intestine into the bloodstream, which delivers them to the rest of the body. Waste products of digestion pass through the large intestine and out of the body as a solid matter called stool.

Did you know that the stomach is only part of your digestive system that absorbs food? The stomach is there to help break down the food into smaller consistency so it is easier for the small intestine to digest the rest. The stomach also releases acids and enzymes for the chemical breakdown of food. After this process, the stomach releases the food into the small intestine. The small intestine is the part of the intestines where 90% of the digestion and absorption of food occurs, the other 10% taking place in the stomach and large intestine. The main function of the small intestine is absorption of nutrients and minerals from food. If the small intestine gets damaged by bad dietary choices, medications, lack of good bacteria, stress etc., you CANNOT absorb nutrients correctly and this can set you up for major chronic illnesses or skin concerns, which I will discuss later.

Did you also know that digestion requires a lot of energy? Some experts estimate that digestion can take 50-80 percent of our total energy. If you are constantly eating all day long, try to stop and give your body a rest and see how you feel. Digestion sucks up so much of our energy, which could be used elsewhere. When the body isn't digesting food, it can go to work on other organs inside the body, healing and regenerating them, which can help us look more beautiful, feel full of life and can also melt away any health issues.

It is also critical that you keep your colon healthy for amazing beauty and health. Your colon (large intestine) is around 5-6 feet long. If you are not eliminating your bowels regularly, toxins can seep into the blood and wreak havoc on your body causing sickness, inflammation, bad skin, premature aging and chronic disease. Ideally, you should be going to the bathroom 2–3 times a day. If you are constipated, this means you are not in a very good state of health or beauty. The longer it takes to empty the bowel, the more unfriendly bacteria takes over and parasites rule. Chronic constipation is the single greatest cause of having an unclean and unhealthy colon and leads to inflammation.

There is a surprisingly wide range of health and beauty problems that colon toxicity contributes to, many that a lot of us experience every day. These include: bloating, constipation, gas, fatigue, food cravings, hypoglycaemia, allergies, arthritis, weight problems, hair loss, acne, eczema and more. If you eat a lot of meat, and/or dairy and are not chewing your food properly, these can become trapped in the colon and may stay there for years – putrefying! Colon cancer is on the rise today and this is why. Your colon is toxic and very inflamed from bad digestion and poor food choices. You need a BIG clean out.

Tips For Keeping Your Colon Clean And Healthy:

1. Eat more fibre-rich foods such as fruits, vegetables and heaps of greens. These act like a vacuum cleaner, sweeping your gut clean.
2. Drink plenty of water.
3. Ensure you have adequate vitamin D. Vitamin D regulates digestion and gut microbes, helping to prevent colon cancer and intestinal permeability (leaky gut).
4. Eat plenty of healthy fats such as coconut oil, avocados, raw seeds etc.
5. Up the GOOD bacteria and digestive enzymes (I will talk more on this later).
6. NEVER suppress the desire to go to the toilet. If you regularly suppress the urge to have a bowel movement, waste materials spend more time than is optimal in your colon, causing excessive dehydration of waste materials and formation of hard stools. This is also a cause of inflammation.
7. Have a colonic irrigation to get rid of toxic waste that may have been hanging around for years. It is one of the best ways to get your colon healthy and clean again. I've done a lot of research on the benefits of colon therapy and enemas and it is all positive. Plus, I have also had a couple and I can tell you I felt amazing afterwards.
8. Eat more chlorophyll rich foods such as wheatgrass, barley grass, spirulina, chlorella and blue-green algae. The high chlorophyll content makes them ideal for colon cleansing. In addition to cleansing, chlorophyll soothes and heals damaged tissue in the digestive tract. It helps the body to obtain more oxygen and draws out toxins.
9. Drink fresh juices and smoothies.
10. Chew your food well.
11. Take aloe vera. This is known to heal the gut.

Ultimately, a clean colon nourishes the body and clears the path to good health and beauty.

> **You cannot be healthy or glowing unless your bowel and colon are clean.**

What Damages Your Gut Health?

- Oral contraceptives – the contraceptive pill is HUGE at wiping out good bacteria. Research suggests that you need double the amount of probiotics if you take the pill.
- Alcohol.
- Sugar and artificial sweeteners. Splenda is packed with chemicals that disrupt the gut's microbiome and causes inflammation. They cause skin problems, weight issues and more.
- Stress – in Chinese Medicine, stress is the root cause of all disease and is just as important as diet. It also wipes out any good bacteria.
- Processed meals.
- Antibiotics/Medications research proves that antibiotics can be extremely harmful to your gut flora. Some antibiotics have been shown to create a lifelong damage in your GI tract. (Remember, I took antibiotics for my acne and then I took the pill, as a consequence my gut was destroyed). Antibiotics are grenades to the gut. They wipe out ALL good bacteria and are now known as another cause of cancer because of this reason. We NEED good bacteria to stay healthy. Antibiotics should only be used in emergency cases.
- Painkillers – these decrease pain in the body but don't actually repair it. They also stop our own natural inflammatory response and that's why there is no healing. They block healing in the intestines, enabling acid to come out, which may cause stomach bleeds or stomach acids.
- Dairy – causes inflammation.
- Gluten – causes chronic inflammation.

- Excess caffeine – very acidic, may also cause inflammation.
- Vegetable oils – another cause of inflammation and very bad for the skin (a cause of acne).
- Preservatives/Emulsifiers – cause inflammation and disrupt the guts microbiome. Look out for carrageenan, xanthan gum, guar gum, locust bean gum, etc. They are bad for our skin and health.
- Lack of sleep – when you are sleep-deprived, your hormones (in particular cortisol) alter, which creates stress within your body and weakens your adrenal system. Also, not getting enough sleep clogs you up. Your colon is just a muscle. If you are tired, your intestinal tract will also be tired.
- Poor digestion – if we don't digest our food properly, then it can create toxins and can overload bad bacteria in our system.
- Heavy metal toxicity – lead, mercury, aluminium, fluoride, chlorine etc. These may come from foods, amalgam fillings, toxic beauty products, toothpastes and more.

I want you to remember this – If your gut is healthy, then you will have a clean slate of beauty and good health.

How To Improve Your Digestion

1. Eat the right foods. This means eating unrefined, chemical/processed free foods that your body is meant to digest and absorb e.g. lots of fresh fruits and vegetables.
2. Take digestive enzymes. These do as the say; they help you to digest food. A bad diet consisting of processed meals will cause us to lose the enzymes we are born with. I will talk more about enzymes later.

3. Improve your absorption of food by healing your gut. Take 2 teaspoons of L-Glutamine powder. One teaspoon at night in room temperature water before bed, and one teaspoon when you wake up. Do this for one month and see how you feel. Take before food.
4. Add probiotics. Supplement from 2 billion up to 100 billion and look for more than 10 strains. The more strains they have the better. Always look for soil based.
5. If your gut is inflamed, you need to eat foods to reduce inflammation such as:

- **Turmeric** – a natural painkiller and anti-inflammatory. Take with coconut oil and black pepper to make it more easily absorbed into your body. This is an important point to note. Turmeric is fat soluble, it must be taken with an oil.
- **Quercetin with Bromelain** – Quercetin is found in red onions, green tea, kale and blueberries. It is a powerful anti-inflammatory. Bromelain is found in pineapples. Having these 2 combinations together, work best as quercetin is easier absorbed with bromelain. Try to eat onions and pineapples every day to heal any inflammation.
- **MSM (Sulphur)** – found in onions, spirulina, garlic and eggs. Sulphur helps to heal a leaky gut and calms inflammation down. You can also buy MSM supplements or in powder form. Powder is best as you can just add to water. The body also absorbs powder more easily than in tablet form.
- **Vitamin C** – is a natural anti-histamine. Histamine is released when the body reacts in an inflammatory way; vitamin C helps to calm this down. Eat more vitamin C rich foods such as acai berries, goji berries, camu camu, baobab, lemons etc.

6. Eliminate any food intolerances. Go and get tested for any intolerance.

7. Eat more soluble and insoluble fibres, for example oats, chia seeds, brown rice, nuts, seeds, and plant based foods.
8. Drink more water. At least 2-3 litres a day.

Chapter 4
Leaky Gut

Otherwise known as 'Increased Intestinal Permeability'.

After all of my years of research, I have finally found the link between my acne and my autoimmune disorder. I had a leaky gut. If I had known I had a leaky gut, I could have healed my acne and I would never have had to have my thyroid destroyed. I believe acne was the first tell-tale sign I had a leaky gut, but as this wasn't addressed, it developed into an autoimmune disorder later on. After years of antibiotics, poor diet, stress, the contraceptive pill, pain killers, heaps of gluten and dairy, it is safe to say my gut was destroyed.

Leaky gut syndrome is a rapidly growing condition that millions of people are struggling with today and don't even know it. From the sound of it, you might think leaky gut syndrome only affects the digestive system, but in reality, it can lead to many other health and beauty conditions as I found out myself. A warning sign that you may have a leaky gut could be something as simple as feeling excessively bloated all day long or chronic brain fog. These are all signs of inflammation. If you do not address the inflammation when you first experience the concern, as time goes on diseases such as autoimmunes may manifest. They say it takes around 4-5 years to finally be diagnosed with an autoimmune disease but the inflammation has been going on for years. Diseases do not just happen overnight.

Let's look at what leaky gut actually means. I want you to imagine looking at your small intestine laid out on the floor. They say it is roughly around the size of a tennis court. Now think of the lining of your digestive tract like a huge net. This net has small holes in it that only allow specific substances to pass through (looks also similar to a cheese cloth). Your gut lining works as a barrier to keep out bigger particles that can damage your system.

When someone has leaky gut, the 'net' in your digestive tract gets damaged, which causes big holes to develop in your net (the cheese cloth has torn), therefore things that normally can't pass through are now able to.

Some of the things that can now pass through include proteins, like gluten, bad bacteria and undigested food particles. Toxic waste can also leak from the inside of your intestinal wall into your bloodstream causing an immune reaction and inflammation.

> **Leaky gut = Fatigued, inflamed and depressed.**

> Healing leaky gut helps to heal your body!

If you have a leaky gut, you WILL have bad gut flora. Good bacteria can help control your gut's permeability. If you had enough beneficial bacteria in your gut, then your gut would be healthy and functioning how it was designed to. A healthy microbiome turns down inflammation. Good bacteria in your gut is IMPERATIVE! You will soon learn why. When your gut flora and gut barrier are damaged, you will be inflamed. Inflammation is the root cause of ALL disease. ESPECIALLY, autoimmune disorders and skin conditions such as acne, psoriasis, eczema and rosacea.

Leaky Gut Symptoms

Leaky gut leads to inflammation throughout your whole system and can cause symptoms/diseases such as:

Bloating/Gas. Digestive problems.	Autism.	Autoimmune diseases.
Candida	Weight gain	Mood Swings / Depression – (gut, brain connection).
Childhood hyperactivity – (ADHD).	Chronic fatigue syndrome or regular fatigue.	Malabsorption – if you eat well and know if you have a nutrient/mineral deficiency, this is a sign you have a leaky gut.
Inflammatory Bowel Disease – (Crohn's, IBS, Celiac Disease, Ulcerative colitis) – all a sign of severe leaky gut.	SIBO (Small Intestinal Bacterial Overgrowth).	Skin concerns like rosacea, acne, eczema, psoriasis and dermatitis – all linked to leaky gut.
Thyroid/ Adrenal issues.	Food sensitivities.	Headaches/Migraines
Diabetes-Type 1.	Joint pain, arthritis or rheumatoid arthritis – research has proven healing your gut heals painful joint conditions.	

If you have any of these symptoms/conditions, then you definitely have some form of leaky gut.

Research also suggests that leaky gut is the cause of more serious conditions such as:

- Alzheimer's disease (linked to a lack of vitamin B12 and omega-3 fatty acids).
- Fibromyalgia.
- Parkinson's disease.
- Multiple sclerosis.
- PCOS (polycystic ovarian syndrome), and so much more.

> One of the biggest warning signs that you may have leaky gut could be that you're experiencing multiple food sensitivities. I recommend that you take a leaky gut test. An intolerance to foods is high indication that you have a leaky gut.

Partially digested protein and fat can seep through your intestinal lining, making their way into your bloodstream and causing an allergic response. This allergic response doesn't mean you'll break out in a rash all over your body, but it can lead to one of the symptoms I mentioned above. If left unrepaired, it can lead to more severe health issues like inflammatory bowel disease, IBS, arthritis, eczema, psoriasis, depression, anxiety, migraine headaches, muscle pain and chronic fatigue.

There is a strong body of evidence pointing to leaky gut syndrome as a major cause of autoimmune diseases, including Type 1 Diabetes. Another problem with leaky gut is that it can cause malabsorption of vital minerals and nutrients including zinc, iron and vitamin B12.

What Causes Leaky Gut?

- Poor diet
- Chronic stress
- Toxin overload
- Gluten / wheat

- Dairy
- Sugar
- Nutritional deficiencies
- Heavy metal toxicity
- Antibiotics/medications
- Bacterial imbalance.

The most common components of food that can damage your intestinal lining are the proteins found in un-sprouted grains such as wheat, rye, and spelt; as well as processed soy, sugar, GMO's and conventional dairy.

Gluten containing grains will damage your intestinal lining and cause leaky gut syndrome. Gluten is an irritating inflammatory substance that can burn the sensitive lining of the intestines. It is one of the biggest causes of inflammation. Also be aware gluten is hidden everywhere. It is added to many foods such as:

- Bouillon stock cubes
- Chewing gum
- Crisps
- Flavoured teas
- Gravies
- Ketchup
- Mayonnaise
- Salad dressings
- Vegetable cooking sprays
- Sweets
- Even some MAKE UP and other beauty products.

Also watch out for labels such as:

- Dextrin
- Malt
- Natural flavourings
- Rice malt or rice syrup
- Whey protein concentrate etc. (a cause of **acne** also).

These also damage the gut, creating inflammation and bad bacterial overgrowth.

Gluten is hidden EVERYWHERE. Basically just avoid processed foods/breads as much as you can! And also use more natural beauty products such as essential oils.

Dairy – conventional cow's milk is another food that can cause leaky gut. The component of dairy that will harm your gut is the protein casein. Also, the pasteurisation process will destroy vital enzymes, making sugars like lactose very difficult to digest. Dairy is believed to cause the same amount of inflammation to the intestinal lining as gluten.

Sugar – wreaks havoc on your digestive system. It feeds the growth of yeast, candida and bad bacteria, which will further damage your gut. Bad bacteria create toxins called exotoxins that damage healthy cells and can eat a hole into your intestinal wall. Sugar fuels inflammation.

I will talk more about dairy and sugar later.

Other Factors That Cause Leaky Gut Are:

- *Chronic stress:* It weakens your immune system, adrenal glands, kidneys and thyroid and over time, this cripples your ability to fight off foreign invaders like bad bacteria and viruses, leading to inflammation and leaky gut. Research has also shown that if you lead a stressful life it can decrease the good bacteria, which then allows yeast to overgrow in the gut. To reduce stress, I recommend:

- Getting more sleep, schedule fun into your week, rest one day a week, meditate, hang out with positive, uplifting people, do yoga or some form of exercise and do things that make you happy.

- Take healing baths with lavender and Epsom salts. A detoxifying bath is always a great way to relieve stress. Plus the Epsom salts are known to boost the lymphatic system and draw toxins out of the body. Epsom salts also contain the mineral magnesium, which is needed to relax the body.

- Drinking nettle leaf, chamomile, liquorice or dandelion tea will also help to calm and relax you, plus they have amazing beauty benefits too.
- *Toxins:* We come into contact with over 80,000 chemicals and toxins every single year, but the worst offenders for causing leaky gut include antibiotics, pesticides, tap water, heavy metals and aspirin. I recommend buying a high-quality water filter to eliminate chlorine and fluoride and look to natural plant-based herbs such as thyme, ashwagandha, turmeric, tulsi tea etc. to reduce inflammation in your body.
- *Medications:* This may be a BIG shock to you but one of the number one causes of leaky gut is prescribed medications. They can deplete the body of nutrients and completely damage the gut lining. Most drugs rob the body of essential vitamins, minerals, antioxidants and good bacteria. This leads to common symptoms such as fatigue, depression, joint pain and so many more deadly diseases. They cause damage to tissues and organs, especially the small intestine, large intestine, stomach and liver. Medications only hide your symptoms they do not get to the root cause of your problem.
- *Dysbiosis*: One of the leading causes of leaky gut is a condition called 'Dysbiosis', which means an imbalance between good and bad bacteria in your gut. For many, this imbalance can begin at birth because of a C-section or because the mother didn't have a healthy gut. It is also due to a lack of enzymes; too little stomach acid; vitamin and mineral deficiencies; food allergies; eating inflammatory foods; a lack of fibre; the overuse of prescription antibiotic drugs; tap water with chlorine and fluoride, and the lack of probiotic and prebiotic-rich foods.

Zonulin

Zonulin is a protein that signals the tight junctions in your 'net' to open and close. Two things that can trigger the release of this protein in the small intestine are gluten and exposure to bad bacteria.

Research suggests it is highly probable that Zonulin is the trigger for intestinal permeability. If the holes in our 'net' stay wide open, then undigested foods slip into the bloodstream, which activates the gut/immune alert. That's when chronic inflammation and disease begin.

Repeated exposure to Zonulin keeps the doors of your net wide open. This lets parasites, yeast, bad bacteria, gluten, and proteins like casein wreak chaos in your body. Your immune system then tries to fight them off. Imagine a war going off in your body. Your immune system is firing at the bad invaders with an imaginary gun to protect you but unfortunately, it also hits your own body tissues, for example your thyroid (but it could be anywhere, even your skin, wherever your weakest link is); this causes your body to start breaking down. Therefore, every time you are exposed to gluten you are opening the holes in your net and if you are repeatedly eating gluten on a daily basis at every meal, the holes in your net WILL NOT close. Those tiny holes will not be tiny neither they will be HUGE. Think about how much gluten you are eating on a daily basis.

Leaky Gut and the Brain

As we mentioned earlier, there is a nerve called the vagus nerve that connects the gut and the brain together. Research is starting to prove that if you can heal the gut you can heal the brain. Leaky gut syndrome has now been linked to other psychological disorders such as anxiety, depression and bipolar disorder and also autism in children. If you've ever seen a child with autism experience a mood swing, this can be caused by intestinal permeability. Gluten-free and casein-free diets have been proven effective for many children with autism because these proteins can leak through the gut and then recirculate and act on the brain.

> **The good news is there's a solution to successfully healing leaky gut.**

1. **REMOVE** foods and factors that damage the gut.
2. **REPLACE** with healing foods.
3. **REPAIR** with specific supplements.
4. **RE-BALANCE** with probiotics.
   BUT it can take from around 6 months to one year to fully heal. You have to be consistent and patient. Your gut did not become inflamed overnight. It may have been inflamed for a VERY long time.

REMEMBER – The top foods to remove that cause leaky gut are:

- **Sugar** – feeds the growth of bad bacteria and yeast, wreaking havoc on the digestive tract. It also causes the skin to age rapidly and is a cause of acne.
- **Gluten** – damages your intestinal lining, causing chronic inflammation.
- **Conventional meat** – meat is pumped with antibiotics today. These antibiotics make their way into our body when we eat the meat, which then destroys our gut. Antibiotics alter the gut microbiome, which causes inflammation.
- **Dairy and GMO foods** – they cause inflammation in the gut the same way as gluten. Avoid GMO crops such as soy, corn, rapeseed, wheat and cotton. These all lead to leaky gut and accelerated aging as well as acne and other skin problems.

The Top Supplements for Healing Leaky Gut

There are many supplements that support your digestive health, but I believe the most beneficial leaky gut supplements are:

- L-glutamine
- Probiotics – A MUST
- Digestive enzymes
- Chlorophyll

- Zinc
- Vitamin B12
- Vitamin A (fat soluble)
- Vitamin D (fat soluble)
- Aloe vera juice
- Quercetin
- Liquorice root
- Collagen powder
- Glucosamine and Chondroitin
- MSM (sulphur) powder
- Frankincense essential oil.
- **L-Glutamine** is critical to heal a leaky gut. Glutamine powder is an essential amino acid supplement that is anti-inflammatory and necessary for the growth and repair of your intestinal lining. L-glutamine benefits include acting as a protector: coating your cell walls and acting as a repellent to irritants. It is known to heal and seal the gut (closing up the holes in the net). Take 2 teaspoons twice a day on an empty stomach in room temperature water. One first thing on waking and second before you go to sleep. You can continue taking for as long as you need. It is an amino acid our body's should have daily.
- **Probiotics** are the MOST important supplement to take because they help replenish good bacteria and crowd out bad bacteria. They also help to calm any inflammation down in the body. I recommend getting probiotics in both food and supplement form. Research is now proving that a lack of good bacteria in the gut is causing autoimmune diseases as well as skin disorders and MORE. Probiotic intake is a MUST.
- Load up on probiotic-rich foods (sauerkraut, kimchi etc.) and take AT LEAST 50 billion units (CFU's) of probiotics daily with 10 strains or more and preferably soil based. Watch out when purchasing for any added emulsifiers/maltodextrins etc. that may have been added to the brand. Remember these disrupt the guts microbiome. You should only need a high dosage of

CFU's while healing your gut, once you heal the gut you may switch to a lower unit.

- **Digestive enzymes** – take 1 or 2 capsules at the beginning of each meal to ensure that foods are fully digested, decreasing the chance that partially digested foods particles and proteins are not damaging your gut wall.

- **Liquorice root** (DGL) is an adaptogenic herb that helps balance cortisol levels and improves acid production in the stomach. DGL supports the body's natural processes for maintaining the mucosal lining of the stomach and duodenum. This herb is especially beneficial if someone's leaky gut is being caused by emotional stress. Take 500 milligrams twice daily or buy liquorice root and chew on it.

- **Quercetin** has also been shown to improve gut barrier function by sealing the gut because it supports creation of tight junction proteins. It also stabilizes mast cells and reduces the release of histamine, which is common in food intolerances. New studies have also shown its effectiveness in healing ulcerative colitis. Take 500 milligrams 3 times daily with meals or eat more quercetin rich foods such as onions.

- **Omega-3 and Omega-6 fats** are important for gut healing and reducing inflammation. Omega-3 fats are found in oily fish and omega-6 fats are found in evening primrose and borage oils. The best vegetarian sources of omega-3 are chia, walnuts, spirulina, kiwi fruit and flax seeds (make sure these are ground).

- **Aloe Vera** juice is very good for digestive health. It helps to reduce inflammation in the gut and may accelerate healing. Having a shot of aloe vera juice every day is a good option for digestive health and beauty. Known to slow down aging.

- **Take Ashwagandha to manage stress** – Ashwagandha is an Ayurvedic herb that lowers cortisol and is known to balance thyroid hormones. It is traditionally used to strengthen the immune system. Also known as an anti-aging herb. It is particularly beneficial for those suffering from thyroid issues as it is known to improve the health of the thyroid; hypo and hyper. It brings your body back into balance.

- **Take vitamin A** – strengthens stomach lining. Ghee is a good source or beta-carotene rich foods such as carrots, sweet potatoes etc. Vitamin A is also a beauty enhancer.
- **Vitamin D3** – reduces inflammation and supports the immune system. Best source is sunshine. Optional take 1000IU. However, I recommend 20 minutes of sunshine per day as your best source.
- **MSM (sulphur)** – this lowers inflammation, raises immunity and fights the effects of stress. A popular joint supplement but it also helps to rebuild the lining of the digestive tract. Helpful to heal a leaky gut. Also used to treat skin conditions such as acne, rosacea and even wrinkles. MSM is necessary for collagen production. You can buy in powder form or naturally it is found in dark leafy greens. See chapter on 'Beauty Minerals' to learn more about sulphur.
- **Collagen powder** – look for marine collagen. Collagen helps to heal the small intestine and of course slows down aging.
- If you are not a vegetarian or vegan; organic bone broth is another option to heal the gut.
- Eat things that are easy on the digestive system such as steamed vegetables, cold-pressed juices and soak nuts and seeds etc. before eating them.
- **Frankincense Essential Oil** – known to help heal an autoimmune condition, it also slows down aging and repairs the gut. Buy in capsules and take internally.

Healing leaky gut can help transform your beauty and health forever!

How To Test If You Have A Leaky Gut:

- Take a breath test. This also detects SIBO.
- Have an organic acid test. This reveals vitamin and mineral deficiencies.
- Have a food allergy test taken.
- Take a stool test. This will tell you the balance of good and bad bacteria in your body.

If you do have a leaky gut, then most likely your liver is also working extra hard to deal with all those toxins floating around your body. Your digestion and colon all link to your liver and if your gut is destroyed your liver will be finding it hard to function well too. One of the consequences of poor liver function is chronic fatigue. Poor digestion, bad food, dysbiosis, gut inflammation and a leaky gut all contribute to chronic fatigue. Eat plenty of artichokes, dandelion greens, lemons, grapefruit and turmeric as they help with liver function. Drinking fresh, cold-pressed, organic celery juice is also known to regenerate the liver and heal the gut.

Stomach acid is also crucial in digestion. Stomach acid is actually critical for mineral absorption. If you do not have enough stomach acid, you will be unable to digest food properly. This disturbs your balance of gut bacteria (dysbiosis). This can lead to indigestion and acid reflux.

One of the biggest causes of low stomach acid is a zinc deficiency because the production of hydrochloric acid is dependent on zinc. Hydrochloric acid usually declines as we age. The symptoms of low stomach acid includes; burping after food, indigestion, flatulence, bloating, diarrhoea or constipation, feeling full after meals straight away or heartburn. Stress also suppresses stomach acid.

Take digestive enzymes containing hydrochloric acid plus zinc citrate if you suffer from low stomach acid.

If you are producing too much stomach acid, then you must be consuming too much meat, fish, eggs, alcohol, painkillers, chilli's, very hot drinks etc. Cut back on these. DO NOT TAKE hydrochloric acid. Simply cut out these and eat more plant-based foods.

Chapter 5
IBS (Irritable Bowel Syndrome)

IBS is also connected to LEAKY GUT!

If you have any or all of the following symptoms continually or recurring for at least 3 months, there is a strong possibility that you may have IBS:

Abdominal pain	Anxiety	Bloating
Cramps	Depression	Mucus in stools
Nausea	Gas	Diarrhoea or constipation

Women also find their symptoms of IBS may worsen around their time of period.

Research Suggests The Main Causes Of IBS are:

- Food allergies, which stems from having a leaky gut as we now know.
- Overgrowth of bacteria in the small intestine.
- Stress (one of the biggest causes of gut issues is stress. Chronic stress makes us sick and inflamed).
- Dietary factors including low fibre consumption.
- A lack of digestive enzymes.
- Parasites living in the gut.
- Zinc or magnesium deficiency.

- Heavy metal toxicity.
- Hormonal imbalances.

Research suggests that it is practically always associated with a food intolerance (once again connects to a leaky gut) as well as dysbiosis (an imbalance in gut flora). Wheat (also in rye and barley), milk and yeast are the biggest culprits.

Care must be taken to heal the gut lining using dietary supplements such as **zinc, vitamin A, essential fats and glutamine** (same protocol to heal the gut).

If you have chronic diarrhoea, then this can result in a zinc deficiency so you will need to supplement with healthy bacteria to normalise your gut and supplement with zinc as well as digestive enzymes.

An overgrowth of yeast, known as candida, sometimes accompanies IBS.

How To Heal IBS – HEAL YOUR GUT!
(Also refer to chapter on leaky gut).

Take:

Zinc – 75mg or 15-30mg.	Magnesium	Digestive Enzymes
Probiotics	**Selenium**	**Herbs to balance hormones (hormones are greatly affected by abnormal bacteria).**
L-Glutamine	Vitamin A	Fish oils to reduce gut inflammation. (Omega-3 DHA/EPA).
Vitamin D3 – 1,000IU-2,000IU.		

1. **Get tested** Try to get a test for food allergies and eliminate the foods that test positive, or simply try an elimination diet for a few weeks and see how you go. No dairy, corn, peanuts, soy, gluten, sugar etc. This is an effective way to isolate the foods that may be causing you problems. The usual culprits will ALWAYS be gluten, dairy and sugar.
2. **Get rid of the unwanted visitors in your small bowel** Repopulate your digestive tract with good bacteria. Take **PROBIOTICS**. People with IBS are most often reported to have a low level of Bifidobacterium. More on this later.
3. **Take digestive enzymes** with meals to help break down food while your gut heals.
4. **Take fish oils, GLA (from evening primrose oil), zinc, vitamin A, aloe vera, l-glutamine, and MSM powder** to help heal the lining of the gut.
5. If you have IBS, this may also be connected to SIBO (small intestinal bacterial overgrowth).

Chapter 6
SIBO
(Small Intestinal Bacterial Overgrowth)

This is a frequent cause of IBS and comes from having a LEAKY GUT

What Is SIBO?

SIBO is the acronym for 'small intestinal bacterial overgrowth', *defined as excessive bad bacteria in the small intestine.*

Overgrowth of these bad bugs' results in the production of bacterial toxins, which can then activate your immune system, which causes damage to the gut wall, inflammation, increased sensitivity, pain, constipation and diarrhoea.

The small intestine is the longest section of the digestive tract *(roughly the size of a tennis court)*. This is where the food intermingles with digestive juices, and the nutrients are absorbed into the bloodstream. **If SIBO is indicated, malabsorption of nutrients, particularly fat-soluble vitamins (A, D, E and K), plus iron can quickly become a problem.**

When in proper balance, the bacterium in the colon helps digest foods and the body absorb essential nutrients. However, when bad bacteria invades and takes over the small intestine, it can lead to poor nutrient absorption, symptoms commonly associated with IBS, and may even lead to damage of the stomach lining. Crohn's, colitis, leaky gut, thyroid issues, autoimmune conditions, excess weight gain etc. are all conditions related to SIBO. The small intestine should not harbour a lot of bad bacteria.

When you have SIBO, as food passes through the small intestine, the bacterial overgrowth interferes with the healthy digestive and absorption process. The bacterium associated with SIBO actually consumes some of the foods and nutrients, leading to unpleasant symptoms, including gas, bloating and pain.

Even when treating small intestinal bacterial overgrowth with antibiotics, relapse rate is high. This is a chronic condition that can be cured, but it takes a lot of patience, perseverance and a complete change in diet. Chronic stress is also a huge cause of this condition; elevated cortisol *(stress hormone)* is a BIG component of SIBO and is worsened by a bad diet and lack of fibre.

Symptoms of SIBO

The indications of SIBO mirror the symptoms of other gastrointestinal disorders, including IBS. **There's a definite association between IBS and SIBO.**

Common Symptoms/Conditions Of SIBO And IBS Include:

Nausea	Bloating	Vomiting	Diarrhoea
Acne	Rashes	Fatigue	Malnutrition
Weight loss	Joint Pain	Anxiety	Depression
Asthma	Rosacea	ADHD (attention deficit disorder)	Alzheimer's
Eczema	Auto-immune diseases	Thyroid	Crohn's

DO THESE SYMPTOMS OR CONDITIONS LOOK FAMILIAR? THEY ARE ALL ROOTED FROM A

LEAKY GUT. TO TREAT SIBO YOU MUST TREAT LEAKY GUT FIRST *(see leaky gut plan).*

Causes of SIBO

There are a number of underlying conditions believed to contribute to small intestinal bacterial overgrowth but the main causes are having a leaky gut, chronic stress, lack of fibre, type 2 diabetes; celiac diseases; eating disorders; autoimmune diseases; certain medications *(antibiotics being the greatest);* diverticulosis and an imbalance of bacteria/dysbiosis.

Aging is also a risk factor for developing SIBO. As we age, the digestive tract slows down.

Complications Associated With SIBO

SIBO, left untreated, can cause potentially serious health complications. It's vital to get rid of the bacterial overgrowth as soon as possible.

Bad bacterial overgrowth in the small intestine can lead to malnutrition. This is one of the biggest concerns with SIBO. Essential nutrients, protein, carbohydrates and fats aren't properly absorbed, causing deficiencies, including:

- Iron deficiency
- Vitamin B12 deficiency
- Calcium deficiency
- Deficiencies in the fat-soluble vitamins, which are:
- Vitamin A
- Vitamin D
- Vitamin E and
- Vitamin K.

These deficiencies can lead to symptoms, including weakness, fatigue, confusion and damage to the central nervous symptom.

Treating SIBO

Small intestinal bacterial overgrowth is most often treated with antibiotics. This will stop any pain and kill off the bad bacteria BUT they will also kill off the healthy bacteria, which is necessary for proper digestive functioning.

Even with antibiotics, SIBO is difficult to treat. As we know antibiotics destroy the gut, which causes inflammation leading to leaky gut. Therefore, if you take antibiotics there is a good chance SIBO will return. Antibiotics DO NOT get to the root cause of the problem. **You have to heal your gut!**

The Best Herbal Remedies For SIBO Are:

- Oregano oil – has shown successful in treating SIBO.
- Berberine extract.
- Wormwood oil.
- Lemon balm oil.
- Indian barberry root extract.
- Sage.
- Allicin from garlic.
- Chinese Skullcap.
- Thyme.
- Neem.
- Cinnamon *(also kills candida)*.
- Dill.
- Pau D'arco.
- Ginger.
- Black walnut *(take in tincture)*.
- Peppermint.
- Caprylic acid from coconut oil (antibacterial, antifungal).

You do not need to consume all of these. Choose a few and see what works.

Tip 1: To help you overcome SIBO consume smaller amounts of food during meals. Spread your meals out at 5-6 smaller portions per day rather than 3. Eating smaller meals allows you to digest foods more quickly, which is crucial to overcoming SIBO. Overeating is one of the worst things for SIBO because it causes food to sit longer in the stomach and can also damage gastric juice production. Low stomach acid production is one of the main contributing factors of SIBO because stomach acid kills off bacteria in your upper GI regions. I would advise eating plenty of unrefined sea salt (this provides chloride, the building block of stomach acid), manuka honey (heals the stomach lining), raw apple cider vinegar (drink on waking in warm water. 1 tsp-1 tbsp. daily or add to meals) and take digestive enzymes. You may also want to think about supplementing with hydrochloric acid with pepsin (this will also help to heal leaky gut) BUT if you are NOT taking protein in a meal, for example meat, you don't need to use it. If you do take it and get warmness in the stomach, that means you are taking enough.

Tip 2: To get rid of SIBO you HAVE to take probiotic supplements and eat probiotic rich foods immediately such as sauerkraut, kimchi etc. Look for bacterial strains such as Lactobacillus casei, Lactobacillus plantarum, Strepetoccous faecalis, Bifidobacterium bevis, and Bacillus coagulans.

THE SIBO DIET

Rid your small intestine of bacteria overgrowth, by going on a FODMAP elimination diet for TWO weeks maximum.

What are FODMAPS? They are foods that aren't fully absorbed in the body and end up fermenting in the digestive tract. The fermentation actually feeds the bacteria, making it more difficult to fight SIBO and SIBO symptoms.

F – Fermentable or creates gas.

O – Oligosaccharides. Found in wheat, garlic, onion, barley, rye and chicory root.

D – Disaccharides. Lactose found in milk, yoghurt and ice cream.

M – Monosaccharide. Sugar fructose. Found in apples, pears, watermelon, honey and agave syrup.

P – Polyols. Sugar alcohols found in peaches, plums, apples, cauliflower, chewing gum and mushrooms.

Foods To Avoid:

- *Fructose* – some fruit and fruit juices, processed honey, cereals, baked goods, high-fructose corn syrup, maple syrup and processed/ refined sugars.
- *Lactose* – conventional dairy and processed products with dairy and added lactose.
- *Fructans* – wheat, garlic, onion, asparagus, leeks, artichokes, broccoli and cabbage.
- *Galactans* – legumes, cabbage, Brussels sprouts, and soy.
- *Polyols* – sorbitol, isomalt, lactitol, maltitol, xylitol and erythritol, commonly found in sugar-free gum, mints and some medications.

Eliminate any irritants and inflammatory foods such as gluten/wheat, dairy, sugar, processed foods, soy, corn oil, hydrogenated oils, sweeteners, emulsifiers, etc.

It is important to stick with a total elimination of the foods on the 'avoid' list.

When you read the list you may wonder what's left to eat. There are plenty of great tasting, healthy foods on the SIBO diet, *don't worry*, PLUS it is only for 2 weeks.

> **The goal of the SIBO diet is to repair the intestinal lining, ease inflammation, get rid of the bacterial overgrowth and eat a diet rich in the essential nutrients that your body hasn't been absorbing.**

During the elimination phase, always keep a supply of foods from the enjoy list with you; you may slip up and if you do, it is suggested to start the 2-week period again. Don't let this happen.

I eat a plant based diet but it is believed that high quality clean proteins, including wild-caught salmon, grass-fed beef, and organic free-range poultry and eggs are needed to heal SIBO as they are easy to digest. However, I don't necessarily agree with this but as I always say listen to YOUR body and see how you feel. You do not have to eat these if you are a vegan like me. You can fuel your body with more plants like dark leafy greens, spirulina, chlorella etc. Juicing them would be a great option as this is easier on the digestive system. You will learn more about juicing and its amazing benefits later. Eating vegetables steamed may also be easier on the digestive tract rather than eating them raw. Again listen to your body.

Eating fresh pineapple daily can help lower inflammation while helping digestion. This is because it is rich in bromelain. Bromelain has amazing health benefits, especially for those with digestive disorders, allergies, asthma and joint pain. I recommend having as a snack or adding to meals, this will also help to break down your food making digestion easier.

Be adventurous and try to eat different foods daily so that you do not get bored. REMEMBER, juicing is also a great option. Here are some foods you can and cannot eat for 2 weeks on the SIBO plan.

What Can I Eat When Healing from SIBO?

Foods to eat	Foods to Avoid
Meat and Fish – Organic, grass fed beef, wild-caught salmon etc. (avoid all processed meats).	Cream / Cream cheese / Soft cheese.
Ghee	Milk / Milk products – ALL dairy.
Eggs – Free range / Organic.	Ice cream
Sprouted nuts and nut butters (avoid pistachios).	Sweetened flavoured yoghurts
Nut milks / coconut milks	Blackberries
Olive oil	Barley
Amaranth	Bulgar wheat
Millet	Couscous
Oats – gluten free	Rye

Quinoa	Semolina
Rice	Wheat and wheat products – ALL gluten.
Aubergine	Artichokes
Carrots	Asparagus
Celery	Avocado
Courgette	Beans and pulses
Green beans	Beetroot
Lettuce	Cabbage
Pak choi	Cauliflower
Peppers	Broccoli
Potatoes / sweet potatoes	Garlic
Spinach	Mushrooms
Spring onion	Onions
Swede	Peas
Cucumber	Sugar snaps and mange-tout
Parsnip	Shallots
Squash	Fennel
Tomatoes	Apples
Bananas	Apricots
Grapes	Peaches
Grapefruit	Cherries
Honeydew melon	Watermelon
Kiwi	Mango
Lemons/Limes	Dried fruits
Oranges	Nectarines
Pineapple	Pear
Rhubarb	Plum
Raspberries/Strawberries/ Blueberries/Cranberries.	Prunes

If you suffer from IBS, this diet may also help to ease symptoms.

**REMEMBER THIS IS ONLY FOR TWO WEEKS.
If you wish to see the FULL FODMAP diet, you can
find it online.**

GAPS Diet (Gut and Psychology Syndrome)

After 2 weeks avoiding FODMAPS, you may wish to transfer to the GAPS DIET. This diet also helps repair LEAKY GUT SYNDROME and IBS. It is known to treat the root cause of MANY gut health related conditions as it helps to rebalance bacteria throughout the digestive tract and prevent toxins entering the bloodstream. This nutritional plan also helps reduce food sensitivities/intolerances, improve neurological function, boost the immune system, reduce anxiety and depression, and HEAL!

There are a number of foods that you need to continue to avoid on this plan. All grains, gluten/wheat, processed sugars, high-starch foods, processed foods, and non-organic meats and dairy. Your system is still healing from SIBO, repairing your digestive tract and getting your body back in balance are the priorities.

GAPS Diet

- Drink one cup of bone broth daily or you can buy bone broth powder and add to smoothies. Another alternative is to take collagen powder in water before each meal or again you can also add to smoothies.
- Use coconut oil or ghee for cooking *(good quality fats).* Coconut oil will help to repair the gut.
- Eat fruit in between meals, NOT with meals.
- Eat probiotic-rich foods (fermented vegetables, kombucha, etc.) Include one forkful with each meal.
- Eat lots of warm soups.
- Eat easily digested vegetables (lightly steamed).
- Drink the juice of fermented vegetables.
- Drink plenty of fresh water throughout the day to stay properly hydrated.

**Incorporate organic, cold-pressed COCONUT OIL
whenever possible during this stage.**

- Also increase your intake of anti-inflammatory foods such as oily fish, olives, chia seeds, flax seeds *(good to balance intestinal tract),* turmeric, and ginger.

Look also for slippery elm tea and charcoal tablets to relieve occasional gas and bloating. Charcoal is known to have amazing detoxifying benefits as it acts like a sponge to toxins in the body. It's your go too, when you have stomach pain, flu, gas etc.

It is also important to manage stress. REMEMBER, chronic stress causes inflammation and bad bacterial overgrowth; we need to keep stress to a minimum. Regular exercise and deep breathing exercises can help reduce stress levels *(see chapter on breathing).* Take up yoga, barre, meditation etc. Also, try other holistic alternative therapies such as acupuncture, reiki, massage, etc. Supplements that may help with anxiety/stress are: passionflower, valerian root, ashwagandha, maca, reishi, holy basil, astragalus, liquorice root or skullcap.

Supplements for SIBO

These help to treat and overcome the nutritional deficiencies caused by SIBO. Follow RDA (recommended daily allowance) levels for each:

- Vitamin B12.
- Vitamin D – best source is always sunshine.
- Vitamin K – also found in dark leafy greens.
- Vitamin A.
- Probiotics – soil based (SBO).
- Digestive Enzymes *(take one before a meal).*
- Iron – can also be found in dark leafy greens.
- Zinc – essential to heal any gut issue.
- Essential fats (omega-3, fish oils, chia seeds, flaxseeds etc.).

Essential Oils for SIBO

In addition to dietary changes and supplements, essential oils have been shown to also be helpful for people with SIBO and other digestive symptoms. Peppermint essential oil is shown to provide relief from certain gastrointestinal symptoms, including IBS and others.

Other essential oils that may be beneficial when treating SIBO include **oregano oil, tarragon oil, frankincense oil, cinnamon, thyme, ginger, turmeric** and **clove oil.** Use only high quality oils, preferably organic. I like Neal's Yard and Young Living. Be sure to use a carrier oil such as fractionated coconut oil. They should NEVER be used neat on the skin or when taken internally. These are powerful digestive supports, not only for SIBO but other inflammatory gut conditions too. You can take internally, mixed in liquid, or use in smoothies. Another great option is to mix with a carrier oil and rub topically on the gut (*see essential oils chapter to learn more about carrier oils).* Lemon and grapefruit essential oils are also known to kill parasites in the gut. Parasites could also be a cause of your SIBO. Look to an essential oils practitioner if you need further advice.

The main goal here is to fix your leaky gut first!

Going low FODMAP will help you control your digestive symptoms but it should NOT be a solution for long term use.

Chapter 7
Food Intolerances

Most people seem to have one these days. Well, guess what? This is also down to the gut – digestion and absorption. If you have a food intolerance, you HAVE to heal the gut. Begin by looking at the foods you are eating and see what may be stressing or irritating the digestive tract. A common cause of food intolerances is inflammation, which is caused by certain foods (gluten and dairy being the main culprits). Research shows people with a food intolerance have leaky gut walls. The gut wall becomes inflamed or damaged and allows undigested foods to enter into the bloodstream. For example, when you have a leaky gut and you eat an apple, instead of the apple being digested it will slip through the holes of your intestinal wall (your net). This apple is now in the bloodstream causing an immune system alert. The apple has become an invader and the immune system starts to fire at the apple to protect you. This causes inflammation and could potentially lead to serious health and beauty issues if you do not heal and seal the gut. The apple is not the problem; you have a LEAKY GUT! Therefore, if you have a food intolerance test and it comes back you are allergic to healthy foods such as fruits and vegetables, this is a clear sign you may have a leaky gut. Our bodies are not designed to be allergic to fruits and vegetables but dairy, sugar and gluten – YES! An interesting fact with people who have a food intolerance is that they can become addicted to the food that is causing the reaction and you may even end up binging on the food that is harming you. My addiction used to be bread. Research suggests that when you are intolerant to a food, the gut releases serotonin (the happy hormone) this then makes the gut move faster and can cause diarrhoea. Most likely the food you are intolerant to is the one you can't live without. Foods such as wheat, dairy and sugar should be avoided PERMANENTLY.

Fortunately, the gut wall can be healed fairly quickly, especially with the amino acid l-glutamine and probiotics.

If You Suspect You Have A Food Intolerance:

- Take a digestive enzyme with each meal.
- Take probiotics twice a day on an empty stomach.
- Look at the foods you are eating and eliminate the bad guys, e.g. gluten, dairy, sugar, trans fats etc.
- Take l-glutamine twice a day on an empty stomach.

Signs of a food intolerance include; bloating, abdominal pain, diarrhoea, indigestion, joint pains, skin concerns, migraines, weight gain, etc.

Chapter 8
Candida

Candida is a condition that can develop when there is an overgrowth of yeast **Candida albicans.** As with every health/skin concern it comes down to the level of good and bad bacteria in your gut. Many different factors cause candida; antibiotics, birth control pills, medications, gluten, sugar, a lack of good bacteria and eating too much processed food.

Candida albicans is the scientific name given to this parasitic fungus that lives inside our gut. Candida is pretty gross; we need to keep its presence in our guts to a minimum. It normally resides in the large intestine but can also migrate into the small intestine and even into the mouth.

Keep in mind that a small amount of candida is normal to have in our gut, gastrointestinal (GI) tract and around our mouth and genitals. A strong immune system and the natural defences of our 'good' bacteria keep this candida in check. That said, if you are pounding your mouth with a diet of processed foods, tons of sugars, gluten, high-glycemic index carbohydrates, then candida will run rampant through your gut and begin to cause a host of illnesses and uncomfortable conditions all throughout your body.

The first element in a candida treatment plan is a low-sugar diet. This is because **sugar is one of the major causes of candida overgrowth,** and our diets today are FULL of sugar! Sugar also fuels bad bacteria. The candida yeast cells need sugar to build their cell walls, expand their colonies and switch into their more virulent, fungal form. A low-sugar diet is a necessary part of your candida treatment as we need to starve the bad bacteria so we can repopulate the good bacteria.

Some Of The Symptoms Include:

Intense sugar cravings	Cravings for bread	Cravings for alcoholic beverages
Menstrual Cramps	Anxiety attacks	Chronic fungal infections of the skin or nails.
Food allergies	Extreme difficulty in losing weight	Excessive bloating or intestinal gas.
Insomnia	Chronic constipation and or diarrhoea.	Excessive emotional outbursts.
Recurring headaches	Mental fog	Joint and muscle pain.

Yeast THRIVES off sugars. You will also need to eliminate ALL dairy products too during your candida cleanse. Dairy contains lactose, which is a form of sugar on which candida love to snack on. Non-organic milk also contains antibiotics that escalate the candida overgrowth. Candida thrives in an acidic/damp environment.

You also have to say goodbye temporarily to fruit, and all yeast-containing foods such as bread, alcohol, peanuts etc.

Getting your intestinal environment back into a healthy state will boost your immune system, improve your digestion, and enhance your nutrient assimilation. This means you will finally be absorbing all the good nutrients from the foods you eat.

Because candida is a fast growing yeast, it can rapidly reproduce after any negative shock to the intestine (for example antibiotics). A course of antibiotics will kill most of your good bacteria, giving the candida yeast an opportunity to rapidly grow and dominate your gut. Candida actually thrives in individuals who take antibiotics. Chances are when you go to the doctor they may prescribe you with antibiotics for this condition. You don't want to do this. Taking antibiotics will further develop a yeast infection.

Probiotics are an effective part of candida treatment because they reintroduce helpful bacteria to your gut. These bacteria create large, healthy colonies that crowd out the candida yeast, regulate your stomach acidity and boost your immune system.

Decide Which Supplements You Need

As I keep mentioning probiotics are an ESSENTIAL part of your diet, it's important to buy a good quality brand. Find one with a high count of bacteria and lots of different strains. Taking a good antifungal will also improve your chances of beating your candida overgrowth. There are lots of natural antifungals to choose from.

First is the cleansing phase. This is when you eat the strictest diet, combined with lots of water and some detox drinks, in order to flush out your colon and quickly eliminate as many of those candida colonies as possible.

During this stage you should be sticking to a diet of raw salads and steamed vegetables, along with various herbs, spices and oils to liven up your meals. It is quite a restrictive diet but you only need to follow it for a few days. You will end the cleanse feeling refreshed, light, healthy and ready to move on to the next stage.

Here is a list of items to include during this cleanse:

1. **Anti-fungals** – you need to take these because the diet and probiotics alone will not be enough to beat your candida overgrowth. Popular antifungal treatments include caprylic acid, grapefruit seed extract, garlic and oil of oregano. You can add antifungals into your diet too, for example, coconut oil is a potent source of caprylic acid, and is also a great oil for cooking at high temperatures with. With so many different health benefits, coconut truly is one of nature's medicines. I'll talk about this later.

2. **Apple cider vinegar (ACV)** – raw ACV is loaded with enzymes that assist digestion and encourages the growth of good bacteria (prebiotic). Because ACV is alkaline forming, it directly helps fight against candida.
3. **Garlic** – is a potent anti-fungal and anti-viral food. Eat lots of this RAW. It is able to slow and kill over 60 types of fungus.
4. **Cucumbers** – contain enzymes that kill parasites. Parasites may also be a cause of candida.
5. **Clove** – a powerful antimicrobial agent.
6. **Cayenne pepper** – destroys fungus and mold.
7. **Onions** – similar to the effects of garlic; onions are a powerful cleanser for the body.
8. **Ginger** – is an ancient detox food with numerous health benefits.
9. **Seaweed** – high in iodine, it helps your thyroid function, assists with oestrogen and candida detoxification, and it can help eliminate toxins and heavy metals from the body.
10. **Lemon and lime juice** – alkalizing and purifying. The juice of lemons and limes are amazing cleansers.
11. **Sage** – anti-microbial.

Supplements To Help Kill Candida:

1. *Grapefruit seed extract* – has powerful properties that are antibiotic, anti-fungal and anti-viral. Can be taken in capsules or as drops. Start with a low dosage and work your way up. DO NOT TAKE DURING PREGNANCY.
2. *Mediterranean oregano oil* – research has shown it to be effective against candida. Capsules should be taken at 1 daily and increased to 2 daily.
3. *Fish oil and krill oil* – besides having various profoundly positive health benefits, omega-3 fatty acids can assist in the elimination of candida.
4. *N-Acetyl Cysteine (NAC)* – this is a potent antioxidant and has proven anti-cancer benefits. Take 400-600mg 2 times daily for 30 days.

5. *Probiotics* – when you are suffering from a candida overgrowth, the microorganisms in your gut are thrown out of balance. Adding a good source of probiotics to your diet (in supplement and through probiotic foods) will repopulate your gut with these helpful organisms. Coconut kefir is a good recommendation for a probiotic rich food. Avoid taking any form of probiotic with a meal or shortly after a meal, as your stomach acid is too strong at this time and most of the live cultures will not survive in your gut, which is where they are needed. **A probiotic is most effective when taken on an empty stomach first thing in the morning or before you sleep.** You need plenty of friendly bacteria to keep the harmful bacteria in check. Probiotics are a MUST with candida.

6. *Aloe Vera* – anti-bacterial and anti-fungal.

7. *Propolis* – known to be effective for all fungal infections of the skin and body.

8. *Tea tree essential oil* – anti-fungal.

9. *Thyme essential oil* – strong anti-microbial action. Make 2% body oil with thyme and coconut oil and apply over abdomen to help treat candida overgrowth.

10. *Myrrh essential oil* – anti-fungal.

11. *Green hulls of black walnut (herb)* – has been shown to kill candida.

12. *Oregon grape root* – kills fungus.

13. *Olive leaf extract* – kills fungus. Begin with 1 capsule daily and increase gradually.

Foods To Eat:

Asparagus	Avocado	Brussels sprouts	Celery
Eggplant/ Aubergine	Courgette	Artichokes	Broccoli
Cucumber	Garlic (raw)	Cabbage	Lemons/Limes

Tomatoes	Olives/ Olive Oil	Onions	Spinach/Kale Dark leafy greens
Chicory Root	**Eggs**	**Coconut Meat**	**Hazelnuts/ Almonds/ Walnuts/ Pecans**
Kefir – dairy free	Millet	Oat bran	Sunflower Seeds / Flax Seeds
Cloves	**Basil**	**Quinoa**	**Buckwheat**
Black Pepper	Dill	Cinnamon	Oregano
Ginger	**Paprika**	**Rosemary**	**Thyme**
Sesame oil / flax oil	Turmeric	Sea Salt	Extra virgin cold-pressed coconut oil
Cinnamon tea	Coconut Aminos	Pepper-mint Tea	Apple Cider Vinegar (RAW, with 'MOTHER', unpasteurised).
Liquorice tea	**Anti-fungal teas: Horsetail, Pau d'arco and Reishi.** **Reishi is a fungus that can fight off nasty things like candida.**		

Eating non-starchy vegetables starves the candida of the sugar that feeds it. You should buy your vegetables fresh and eat them raw, steamed or grilled.
AVOID starchy vegetables such as sweet potatoes, potatoes, yams, corn, all winter squash, beets, peas, parsnips and beans.
Olives are OK as long as they are not in distilled white vinegar.

Foods To Avoid:

Artificial sweeteners, including diet/regular sodas and energy drinks.	Bread/ Gluten.	Canned, processed and microwaved foods.
All fruit and fruit juices. Canned fruit and dried fruit.	All forms of sugar (including honey, molasses, syrup, rice syrup And yes chocolate too).	All dairy – cheese, milk, whey etc.
Refined or heated oils (except coconut oil).	Soy	Alcohol
Beans/Legumes	Fried foods	Pistachios/ Peanuts.
Also watch out for things like ketchup, tomato paste and spaghetti sauces, all contain hidden sugars.	Black and Green Tea / Coffee.	Table salt
All pork products	Preservatives such as citric acid.	Potatoes/Sweet Potatoes/Yams/Parsnips/ Carrots/Peas/Beets/ Mushrooms.

Condiments tend to be high in sugar and can exacerbate your candida. Always read food labels to make sure your food doesn't contain sugar. Be careful – the aspartame in diet cola weakens your immune system, destroys beneficial bacteria and can leave you vulnerable to candida.

- **Alcohol** consumption tends to decrease the effectiveness of insulin, leading to consistently higher blood sugar levels. Alcohol can also increase gut permeability and negatively affect your immune system.
- **Caffeine** can cause your blood sugar to rise, but the main problem is that it weakens the adrenals and can impair your immune system. Coffee also contains mold. Mold grows candida. Even decaf tea and coffee are to be avoided as they contain residual levels of caffeine.
- **Mushrooms** eating some fungi can cause an inflammatory reaction if you are already suffering from candida. However, some medicinal mushrooms are actually okay on the diet and have strong immune boosting properties. Good examples are reishi and maitake.
- **Vinegar** is made in a yeast culture, depletes the stomach of acids and can also cause inflammation in your gut. However, one particular vinegar RAW unpasteurized apple cider vinegar with 'The Mother' can be helpful in combating a candida overgrowth.
- Peanut, corn and canola oil are contaminated with mold, and most soy beans used in soy oil are GMO (genetically modified).

Try to drink this shot every morning or between lunch and dinner to combat your candida:

- Half a squeezed lemon.
- A quarter teaspoon of turmeric powder.
- A quarter teaspoon of ground black pepper (only use peppercorns, not the powder).
- A quarter teaspoon of ground cayenne pepper.
- Five drops of organic grapefruit seed extract (GSE), or one tablet of GSE.

An Ideal Day on the Candida Cleanse

First Thing	Take 1 probiotic on waking, and then wait 15-20 minutes to take 2 tbsp. of apple cider vinegar mixed with ½ lemon juice squeezed in warm water.
Breakfast	Green Smoothie (no fruit).
Lunch	Large green salad. Followed by green vegetables.
Snack	Green Juice or Green Smoothie (no fruit).
Dinner	Begin with a large green salad followed by homemade broccoli soup.
You may shot 1tbsp of ACV before meals or the shot I mentioned earlier.	

It's not a good idea go back to your original diet. That diet probably caused your candida overgrowth. Learn to balance your life with more of the good stuff to crowd out the bad. The key here to keep candida at bay is to keep your gut flourishing in GOOD bacteria.

Chapter 9

Parasites

Symptoms of Parasite Infestation

Constipation/Diarrhoea	Skin eruptions e.g. acne
Digestive disorders (even autoimmune diseases)	Chronic fatigue
Irritability/Nervousness	Disturbed sleep
Irritable bowel syndrome	Anaemia
Persistent skin problems	Muscle cramps
Sugar cravings	Joint pains
Ravenous appetite	Craving dirt, clay, raw rice, dried foods, charcoal/burned food
Allergies/Intolerances	SIBO
Nasal itching, picking	Bluish specs in whites of eyes
Coin size blotches on face	Feeling bloated

Parasites can live in our digestive system when the bowels are not moving frequently enough. Parasites also feed on your food so can make you malnourished. Nutritional deficiencies are also a cause of autoimmunity, skin conditions and other chronic diseases. The primary source of parasites come from meat and raw fish (sushi).

Carnivores like lions have a short digestive tract. In a carnivore's digestive tract, the parasite larvae in meat and fish are not able to hatch as easily, because the food moves out in 3–8 hours. Humans have a long, plant-friendly digestive tract and it can take 17–24 hours (or 2–3 days if we are unhealthy) to move food through our system, which then allows time for parasite larvae to hatch.

It is important that everyone does a parasite cleanse at some point in their life. This may consist of a combination of various anti-parasite herbs taken daily. These herbs primarily include raw garlic, aged garlic extracts, as well as whole powdered wormwood, cloves and black walnut hull.

Parasite Killers

Hot peppers	Onion	Green apples	Fennel seed	Oregano oil
Olive leaf extract	Aloe Vera	Thyme	Myrrh	Cloves
Rhubarb	Pumpkin seeds	Garlic	Cucumbers contain enzymes that kill tapeworms.	Cayenne pepper destroys fungus, mold and parasites.
Probiotics are also EXTREMELY affective at combating parasites, fungus, mold and yeasts in the body and digestive tract.				

Parasites are also a cause of chronic inflammation in the gut and may be another reason why you are suffering from a skin problem, digestive issue or chronic illness.

Another effective remedy to help remove parasites is via colonic hydrotherapy.

Chapter 10
Stress and the Gut

I believe the majority of the population today are stressed. What we don't realise is that it is seriously damaging to our health and beauty. Chronic stress may lead to heart disease, obesity, diabetes, weight gain, hormonal problems, rapid aging, autoimmune diseases and more; research has shown that stress is just as toxic for you as having a bad diet plus it is also a cause of acne. Stress causes excess sebum to be produced, which may result in a flare up.

Being stressed shuts down your digestion and creates inflammation in the gut. HAPPY NEWS though research has proven that if you take probiotics and digestive enzymes they reduce the stress response.

The bacteria in your body know when you are stressed out. If you are stressed a lot you are unable to absorb nutrients from food, oxygen is reduced to get to the organs, the blood cannot flow properly and you have less enzymes in the gut. Stress wreaks havoc on your adrenals, kidneys, thyroid gland and leads to digestive issues.

Two of the worst food factors for stress are caffeine and alcohol. Try to cut down on them both. They cause inflammation in the body and can overtax your organs.

Take in more foods that heal and help with stress such as foods containing vitamin B12, omega-3 fatty acids, foods rich in magnesium and calcium; adaptogenic herbs such as ashwagandha, maca, chamomile, chaga, tulsi, green tea, liquorice root and ginseng.

It is important that you learn how to manage stress as it can have a negative impact on the gut microbiome. The more stressed you are, the less good bacteria you will have, and this triggers chronic inflammation. As a cause skin conditions such as acne, eczema etc. can also be triggered or amplified.

Stress is also known to promote fat storage around the belly area and it breaks down collagen in the skin, which leads to rapid aging. Chronic stress really is bad news.

To help with stress do yoga or any other form of exercise. Exercise is one of the best stress busters out there. Meditate, pray, go to the beach, take a walk and ground yourself in nature, journal daily, inhale calming essential oils such as lavender or neroli, switch your phone off, reduce interaction with negative people, listen to music; do things that make you feel happy and good.

Also increase your intake of PROBIOTICS and ENZYMES. These will help to decrease any inflammation.

And pay attention to your posture. Stand up straight and tall. Carry yourself well with confidence. If your shoulders are hunched over and your back is rounding, it is difficult for oxygen to flow freely into your heart and around your body. You're suffocating your heart. The more oxygen that can get around your body the less stressed you can feel. Open your chest more and just breathe. One of my favourite yoga poses for this is camel.

Chapter 11
The Role of Probiotics and Prebiotics

Believe it or not but we are mainly made up of just bacteria.

> **"If you were to take away the water in our bodies, you'd be left with mostly dirt made of sixty of the most abundant elements in the Earth's crust. We are made from mud. We are an amalgam of the Earth's elements: oxygen, hydrogen, carbon, nitrogen, calcium and phosphorous with traces of potassium, sulphur, sodium, iron and magnesium. All of these elements come together to make a living breathing human being." – Dr Josh Axe**

In our guts and on our skin we have bacteria (a microbiome). The health of your microbiome determines how healthy you are. If your microbiome is unhealthy, then chances are high you will have bad skin and bad health. The missing link to all of our health and beauty worries today is with the health of your microbiome.

We need dirt in our diets to survive. Dirt from the Earth. Naturally, we should be eating dirt from the soil. This is where all the good bacteria is, however; unfortunately, today we aren't getting it. Our green leaves that we buy from the supermarkets come in packaged bags washed heavily in chlorine, which are destroying our guts and all the good bacteria has been washed away. We have become obsessed with cleanliness. In an ideal world, we would be picking our produce from the ground with the soil still intact. The soil is where the good bacteria and minerals are, we need that to be healthy and beautiful. WE

NEED BACTERIA and WE NEED MINERALS. Both of which we are lacking in today.

So as we can't get the good bacteria from our produce and soils anymore we need a little helping hand. This is where probiotics come in.

Let's have a look to see why they are SO IMPORTANT.

Probiotics strengthen your immune system and keep your digestive system happy and healthy. They live inside your GI tract. They aid in digestion by cleaning out your gut so that all things keep flowing. You cannot nourish yourself effectively without them. These probiotics/good bacteria determine things such as whether you have glowing skin, whether you are able to lose weight and even if you will develop an autoimmune condition. We need these bacteria for EVERYTHING!

Probiotics also need to be fed in order to remain active and healthy. They are fed by prebiotics. If probiotics do not have enough prebiotics to feed on them, they may also feed on your intestinal lining, which is another cause of leaky gut. Prebiotics are a type of fibre that live inside the large intestine. The more prebiotics that probiotics have to eat the more efficiently these live bacteria work and the healthier your gut will be. Without fibre, bad bacteria will grow.

As I mentioned earlier, probiotics are naturally found in our soils where we get our vegetables from, however due to the pesticides our soils are being sprayed with today we have lost all of the goodness in our dirt. Good soil helps to supply specific vitamins, natural antibiotics, amino acids and phytochemicals vital to our beauty and health.

Probiotics also support the liver in detoxification, the kidneys in cleansing, and the bowel in elimination. Probiotics are known to help lift mood and can help fight anxiety or depression (remember the vagus nerve connection).

Probiotics increase levels of vitamin B12 by improving nutrient absorption. Vitamin B12 plays a vital role in the normal functioning of the brain and the nervous system and in the formation of red blood cells. It also helps to regulate and synthesize DNA. It is needed in the metabolism of every cell in the body, and it plays a part in the synthesis of fatty acids and energy production. By helping the human body to absorb folic acid, it facilitates the release of energy.

The human body produces millions of red blood cells every minute, but without vitamin B12, cells cannot multiply properly. The production of red blood cells goes down if a person's vitamin B12 levels are too low. As the red blood cell count drops, anaemia, fatigue, or depression may set in, or a long term deficiency can cause permanent damage to the brain and central nervous system. B12 should be found to some extent in soil and plants; however, as mentioned earlier due to our soils depletion today I very much doubt it is still there. Only bacteria can manufacture vitamin B12. Foods high in vitamin B12 include, eggs, yeast extracts such as marmite, and nutritional yeast (but make sure they state added B12 on the label), also known to be in spirulina and chlorella too, (however, research suggests that we cannot absorb the B12 from these sources).

A good probiotic supplement can take over the intestinal tract, crowding out disease-causing bacteria, viruses and yeasts. Using probiotics has also been proven to help with skin disorders such as **acne, eczema, rosacea** and **psoriasis.**

Choosing a Good Probiotic

- Purchase a probiotic brand that has a high number of probiotics, ranging from 6 billion to a 100 billion (CFU's).
- Look for a probiotic that has 10 or more strains. The more strains the better.
- Look for strains like Lactobacillus plantarum, Bacillus subtilis, Saccharomyces boulardii, mushroom mycelia and phages to ensure that the probiotics make it to the gut and are able to colonize. Some of these strains also help in the quest to decrease acne.
- Good bacteria to look for – Acidophilus, Bifidobacterium bifidum and Saccharomyces boulardii are some strains known to heal the gut.
- Always buy from the fridge if you can but not a necessity.
- Try to buy a soil based probiotic and one that can pass through your stomach acid.
- Probiotics in liquid form are another great option.

- Eat fermented foods such as sauerkraut, coconut kefir, raw goats' milk kefir etc.

IT IS IMPORTANT TO REMEMBER TO TAKE A LARGE DIVERSITY OF PROBIOTIC STRAINS IN YOUR GUT, BECAUSE EACH ORGANISM SERVES A DIFFERENT PURPOSE.

Probiotic Strains

The bacteria in your gut have a HUGE impact on your health and beauty. They affect how well you digest food; absorb nutrients, metabolism, the strength of your immune system, they prevent inflammation as well as calm inflammation, they are now known as the secret to beautiful skin and lustrous hair and they keep your small intestine and colon very happy. The bacteria in your gut are a community and there are many types, or strains, of bacteria that make up that community. We need these different strains for good health and gorgeous skin. Let's have a look at SOME of the best probiotic strains for supporting gut health and beauty.

1. **Streptococcus Thermophiles** – promotes healthy tissue in the small intestine. It discourages nitrates, like those in celery, spinach, and cured meats from turning into harmful nitrites. It also breaks down a protein in cheeses, casein, which is known to cause allergies and acne.
2. **Bacillus Laterosporus** – fights candida and other types of harmful organisms.
3. **Pediococcus Acidilactici** – undigested food can rot in your gut, which causes inflammation. This bacterial strain helps put a stop to that. It is also known to help keep harmful organisms from damaging the gut environment.
4. **Bifidobacterium Breve** – is ESSENTIAL for colon health, especially if you have taken antibiotics. Studies have found that many digestive problems coincide with low levels of this bacterium. It helps to crowd out the bad bacteria, which is a must.

5. **Bifidobacterium Infantis** – supports the digestive system by releasing an acid that keeps harmful organisms from taking hold. It is especially helpful for people suffering from digestive ailments, constipation and is known to alleviate IBS.

6. **Bifidobacterium Bifidum** – keeps bad bacteria out, eases digestion and boosts the immune system. An important strain as it helps with immune function and allergy response; and it encourages healthy, clear skin.

7. **Bifidobacterium Lactis** – neutralizes gliadin, the wheat protein responsible for gluten sensitivity. Gliadin also damages the intestinal lining and is another cause of leaky gut.

8. **Bifidobacterium Longum** – keeps acid levels balanced. Supports liver function, reduces inflammation and removes heavy metals such as mercury, lead etc. from the body. This is a good strain for anyone taking antibiotics.

9. **Lactobacillus Acidophilus** – one of the most known strains. It supports digestion, and boosts the immune system. This bacterium colonizes in the small intestine, where it helps maintain the integrity of the intestinal wall, ensuring proper nutrient absorption, and supports healthy digestive function. This strain also supports vaginal health in women and is known to help create vitamin K. Vitamin K is a beauty enhancer, therefore a good strain to include for healthy skin.

10. **Lactobacillus Brevis** – is soothing to both oral and colon tissue.

11. **Lactobacillus Bulgaricus** – creates natural antibiotics in your gut that fight invading organisms. It also releases acids that neutralize toxins and promote balance.

12. **Lactobacillus Casei** – supports digestion, boosts immune system, and soothes the bowels.

13. **Lactobacillus Gasseri** – supports digestive health, balances blood sugar, and encourages a healthy body weight. This strain is predominantly linked to the microflora in the vagina. Women with vaginal discomfort usually have lower levels of this bacterial strain.

14. **Lactococcus Lactis** – helps digestion and encourages a healthy gut environment. A good strain to defend against leaky gut.
15. **Lactobacillus Plantarum** – you may want to look for this strain if you have **acne** or **rosacea** as it is known to decrease flare ups. A good anti-inflammatory strain that may also help with premature aging. It produces L-lysine, an amino acid that supports calcium absorption, hormone production, and boosts the immune system. It is often used as a remedy for bowel disorders.
16. **Lactobacillus Paracasei** – anti-inflammatory. Reduces the risk of many skin disorders. May help with **rosacea, eczema** or **dry skin**. A good strain for fatigue, it protects teeth from cavities, and it is known to lessen the impact of environmental toxins. It is found in the small intestine and has the ability to support a healthy liver function. If your liver is healthy, this will show on your skin.
17. **Lactobacillus Rhamnosus** – known to promote a happy and healthy gut environment. Helps with UTI's by kick-starting antibodies and boosting the immune system. Another beneficial strain for vaginal health and supports healthy skin. May also help reduce eczema in babies.
18. **Lactobacillus Salivarius** – fights unwanted microbes in the mouth and the small intestine. A good strain for oral health. This bacterium is known to thrive on prebiotic foods like barley, bananas, tomatoes and garlic. It is found in the oral cavities (mouth, throat, and sinuses), intestines, and vagina, but grows best in the small intestine. Very powerful at cleansing the colon and boosting the immune system. It also prevents any bad bacteria from taking over the gut.
19. **Lactobacillus Fermentum** – this strain is found in probiotic foods such as kimchi and sourdough, it produces superoxide dismutase and glutathione; both powerful antioxidants that help neutralize some of the toxic products made in the gut during digestion. A great strain for good digestion and detoxification.
20. **Lactobacillus Reuteri** – is found in the intestine and oral cavity. Supports digestive, oral, and immune health.

Bifidobacterium Species

Billions of Bifidobacterium line the walls of the large intestine (colon) and help ward off intrusive harmful bacteria and other microorganisms, including yeast. Like the Lactobacillus strain, Bifidobacterium produce lactic acid, which provides up to 70 percent of the energy required by cells that line the intestinal wall, enhancing the natural protective barrier in the gut. Lactic acid also helps keep the pH of the large intestine acidic to discourage the growth of bad bacteria. Additionally, this lower pH environment facilitates the absorption of minerals such as calcium, copper, magnesium, iron, and zinc. Bifidobacterium also produce B-complex vitamins and vitamin K. As we age, the numbers of Bifidobacterium found lining the large intestinal wall naturally begins to decline.

1. **B. Bifidum** – this probiotic strain is among the first to colonize in the intestines of babies and continues throughout life to be one of the main groups of good flora found in the large intestine. (It can also be found in the small intestine). In addition to helping promote bacterial balance, it prevents the growth of unwanted bacteria, molds and yeasts. B. Bifidum assists in the breakdown of complex carbohydrates, fat, and proteins during digestion. It also produces enzymes that break the larger molecules down into smaller components that the body can use more efficiently. Very beneficial for leaky gut. It is one of the probiotic strains that can help alleviate occasional diarrhoea, especially when travelling.

2. **B. Longum** – is one of the more common strains of Bifidobacteria found in the GI tract. Its digestive benefits stem from its ability to break down carbohydrates and to scavenge and neutralize everyday toxins found in the gut. Research suggests that the antioxidant properties of this strain include the chelation of metal ions, especially copper and the scavenging of free radicals. It is also supports a healthy immune system and overall digestion and detoxification.

3. **B. Infantis** – this probiotic strain is the largest population of beneficial bacteria in babies. The amount of B. infantis in our guts decline as we age, but it remains an important part of our microflora. Supplementation with B. infantis has been shown to decrease bloating and bowel movement difficulty.
4. **B. Coagulans** – improves the body's ability to use calcium, phosphorus, and iron. This strain also supports vaginal health in women.
5. **B. Breve** – anti-inflammatory. Protects against UV damage to the skin, minimizing sun spots, wrinkles etc.

Streptococcus Species

1. **S. Salivarius K12** – this probiotic strain is found in the oral cavity's mucus membranes and is known for its ability to produce BLIS (bacteriocin-like inhibitory substances), which inhibit the ability of bad bacteria to grow. Research has found that people who naturally carry BLIS-producing strains of oral bacteria have significantly fewer sore throats (strep throat). Studies have also associated this strain with better ear health and less ear infections in children *(avoid giving children antibiotics for ear infections. This could cause later health problems such as autoimmune conditions etc. Give them probiotics instead)*. This strain also helps reduce dental plaque, and significantly reduces bad breath. May also combat **acne.**
2. **S. Salivarius M18** – is found predominantly in oral mucosa and, like the K12 strain, it also produces BLIS. This bacterium is most active in specific areas on the gums and teeth and promotes healthy gums. If you suffer from gum disease, it may be linked to a lack of good bacteria in the gut.

Most experts believe the average healthy mix of microbes is around 80% good and 15% bad. This creates balance.

This is just an idea of what SOME of the strains of bacteria do. There are more strains, which I have not covered but I hope you can see how important the gut's eco-system is. The latest research reveals that the health of the microbiome has a direct impact on EVERYTHING from oral health, to metabolism, to skin health, to digestion, to autoimmunity and so much more.

When you are looking for a probiotic brand to purchase always look for 10 or more strains. The more strains they have the better. As you can see each strain has a particular role to play in the body. The more strains we can take in the better this will be for our skin and our health.

A toxic gut leads to: chronic illnesses, bad skin, premature aging and more. It is imperative we boost the gut with GOOD bacteria to turn inflammation down in the body. Inflammation is the root cause of ALL!

Probiotic Rich Foods

1. **Kefir** – actually means to feel good in Turkey. Contains beneficial bacteria and yeasts. Also contains lactic acid, which is an anti-aging ingredient. You can make yourself, from raw grass fed milk, preferably goats or my favourite is from coconuts. You can make with coconut cream, coconut water or coconut meat. Try to avoid the dairy kind if you can.

2. **Sauerkraut** – fermented cabbage. Take 1 forkful before each meal or with food. Eat every day. Research says in one forkful this contains more CFU's than a FULL bottle of probiotics (recipe also in the final chapter).

3. **Kimchi** – (a Korean spicy cabbage) it is loaded with antioxidants and boosts the immune system, helping you to absorb nutrients. Amazing for your gut, your heart and every part of your body.

4. **Kombucha** – make this cultured tea at home or you can buy at the store. Contains probiotics, enzymes, vitamins and polyphenolic antioxidants (also helps the brain).

5. **Apple Cider Vinegar** – actually a prebiotic but it helps you to produce your own probiotics in the gut. Take 1 tsp. – 2 tbsp. a day mixed in water or add some raw honey. Another great option is to drizzle over your salads. ACV will cure anything. It is amazing stuff.

6. **Tempeh** – fermented soy. Fermented soy is the only soy you are allowed to eat.
7. **Miso** – has beneficial bacteria's and yeast. Good source of B vitamins.

Prebiotic Rich Foods

Raw Chicory Root	Raw Jerusalem Artichoke
Raw dandelion greens	Raw garlic
Raw onions	Cooked onions
Raw asparagus	Raw banana
Cabbage	Root veg. e.g. sweet potato, carrots, beets, turnips, parsnips etc.
Apples (pectin feeds good bacteria).	Avocados
Blueberries	Broccoli
Brussels sprouts	Celery
Chia seeds	Cucumbers
Figs	Flaxseeds
Greens	Hemp seeds
Kale	Lentils
Oats	Pears
Raspberries	Sesame seeds
Strawberries	Spinach
ALL DARK LEAFY GREENS	**FRUITS AND VEGETBALES**

The less they are heated the more they will retain that healthy prebiotic fibre. Always try to eat raw.
A PREBIOTIC IS FIBRE.

Chapter 12
Probiotics for Beauty

Research has found that the health of your skin is down to the health of your microbiome. If your skin is inflamed, then it is very likely your gut is inflamed too.

- **Probiotics can help keep you slim.** Microflora reduces cravings for carbohydrates, sugar and alcohol. New research has found that obese people have different bacteria in their intestines than people of normal weight. The health of the microbiome is closely linked to obesity.
- **Probiotics clean your liver.** Traditional Chinese Medicine teaches that the liver affects your skin and eyes. With a clean liver, you may notice younger looking skin, bright, shiny eyes and less liver spots, moles and skin tags.
- **Probiotics treat acne.** Certain strains of bacteria heal skin conditions like acne, rosacea and eczema. Whatever probiotic is treated for acne usually works with other skin problems too.
- **Probiotics can prevent wrinkles.** Good bacteria in your gut can help you eliminate the toxins and free radicals that can damage skin and cause early signs of aging.
- **Probiotics give you a glowing complexion.** Probiotics help you digest and better assimilate the nutrients from your food. That means your skin receives more of the antioxidants, vitamins and minerals it needs to be healthy.

- **Probiotics help your hair grow long and lustrous.** Hair may be dead, but each hair follicle is surrounded by nourishing blood vessels. Beneficial microflora help keep your intestines clean and healthy. Healthy blood nourishes hair, skin and nails.
- **Probiotics make your fingernails stronger.** Nails are made of proteins, and probiotics break down the proteins you eat into the amino acids that build healthy, flexible nails.
- **Probiotics give you energy.** It's much harder to look and feel good when you're tired, but consuming probiotics boosts your immunity and makes digestion easier, giving you more energy to look amazing.
- **Moisturise.** Probiotics help skin to maintain moisture. Streptococcus thermophiles has been found to increase moisture in the skin of aging women.
- **Sun Damage.** Probiotics can help protect skin against damaging UV rays that can cause premature skin aging and wrinkles.

Chapter 13
Digestive Enzymes

Ann Wigmore, the mother of the raw-foods movement in America, says that **"enzyme preservation is the secret to health"**.

Enzymes are living, biochemical factors that activate and carry out all the biological processes in the body, such as digestion, nerve impulses, the detoxification process, nutrient absorption and transportation, hormone production, the functioning of RNA/DNA, repairing and healing the body and so much more.

All chronic disease originates in the gut. Even premature aging is caused by a damaged gut.

If you have any type of digestive problem such as acid reflux, gas, bloating, Crohn's disease, ulcerative colitis, constipation etc., digestive enzymes will help you.

We are all born with a bank account of enzymes, however, overtime we begin to lose this bank account and slowly this causes aging as well as chronic illnesses.

We lose our bank account of enzymes through the unhealthy food choices we make on a daily basis. When you eat foods that do not contain enzymes, for example, overheated or processed meals with zero enzymes, then your body must work over time to produce the enzymes it needs to maintain good health. The longer you deny your body of healthy food enzymes, the more exhausted it becomes and the less it is able to produce the enzymes on its own. The body is then set up for future disease and sickness.

Enzymes also as mentioned above play a key role in detoxification. Therefore, when you do not get enough enzymes, the body is unable to remove toxic waste and the more toxins you have in the body again the more you are setting yourself up for future health concerns. Enzymes are necessary for life.

Along with helping to detoxify your body enzymes also help to give you your glow back! They prevent greying of the hair, heal acne, give you heaps of energy, repair your DNA, help digest our food, prevent wrinkles, giving us more youthful skin, may even help your hair grow in faster and stronger and they can help speed up weight loss as they free up more metabolic energy. A great way to get these enzymes in is by juicing, more on that later.

> **Enzymes can reverse the aging process and increase our beauty and health.**

Tip – If you are suffering from indigestion, simply take a digestive enzyme supplement with each meal. Look for ones that provide:

- Amylase – digests carbs.
- Invertase – digests sugars.
- Protease – digests protein.
- Lipase – digests fat.
- Glucoamylase – digests greens.
- Alpha-galactosidase – digests pulses.

Where Do I Get Enzymes From?

Eating raw food is the number-one activity, which preserves enzymes and maximizes health and beauty. Raw fruits and vegetables are packed with enzymes. Be sure to eat a great deal of raw, organic fruits and vegetables on a daily basis, as well as raw nuts and seeds. Eat as many raw veggies as you can at every meal. Especially GREEN! Without enzymes, there would be no life in our cells.

Start each day with a green smoothie or green juice.

Always chew your food well to release enzymes and make them readily available for use in your body.

Reasons to Take Enzymes:

1. Anyone eating cooked, microwaved, processed food should take food enzyme supplements to compensate for the lost and destroyed naturally occurring food enzymes that were previously in the food. Heat destroys enzymes.
2. As we age, we naturally lose enzymes so they may need to be topped up. Eat more fruits and vegetables or even better start juicing them.
3. During acute and chronic illnesses, there is often an enzyme depletion that can be alleviated by enzyme supplementation or once again start juicing. Juicing allows the enzymes to go straight into your blood. Juicing is a great thing to do if you are suffering from any chronic illness.
4. Enzyme supplementation can be a big support to the immune system.
5. Enzymes help to detoxify the body and they help to break down food into smaller particles.

High Enzyme Food

Coconuts	Bananas
Papaya	Lemons
Apples	Wheatgrass
Cucumbers	Avocados
Ginger	Mangoes
Sprouts	Grapes
Parsley	Watermelon
Raw Honey	Bee Pollen
Pineapple	Raw Fruits and Vegetables

> Research suggests enzymes balance and enhance the immune system; helping to heal cancer, multiple sclerosis, rheumatoid diseases, and arthritis; minimize the effect of athletic injuries; decrease injury recovery time; and aid with digestion.

The skin is nourished by a diet rich in enzymes. Enzymes are needed for beauty.

The more enzymes we have in our diet, the easier time the body has with digestion and metabolism.

ENZYMES ARE THE SPARK OF LIFE. We need them to survive.

Chapter 14
The Importance of Detoxing

Detoxification means cleansing the blood.
Today, with more toxins in the environment than ever, it is
critical to detox / clean out!

**We clean our homes, cars and clothes and yet we very
rarely take care of our inner home. Over the years
debris and toxins accumulate in our cells, especially
fat cells, blood, liver and gut, which leads to ill health,
premature aging and bad skin.**

A Clean Body Is a Glowing,
Strong and Healthy Body!

If you are suffering from any of these symptoms:

Unexplained fatigue	Spots/Acne
Sluggish elimination	Irritated skin
Allergies	Puffy eyes or bags under the eyes
Bloating	Menstrual problems

Mental confusion	Excess weight
Coated tongue	Headaches
Dull hair or skin	Lethargy

Then I would suggest you do a detox/cleanse!

Detoxification is one of the body's most basic functions of eliminating and neutralising toxins through the colon, liver, kidneys, lungs, lymph and skin. However, even if your diet is good, a spring cleanse can revitalise your system and rid your body of harmful bacteria, viruses and parasites.

Cleansing the colon is an important part of the detoxing process because those toxins need to exit the body and if your colon is packed with food, toxins can be reintroduced back into the blood stream, rather than exiting. When you detox the body you free up your organs to function the way they should.

Detoxing/Cleansing is one of the most important ways to achieve high levels of health, beauty, reverse aging, and lose weight.

We cannot rebuild, heal or maintain our weight easily without cleansing. Detoxing cleans out the sludge and mucus in our bodies so we can fully absorb nutrients and minerals. Toxicity becomes lodged in our cells and tissues from years of improper digestion, preservatives in our food, chemicals in our skin care products, pollution in the air we breathe and stress. We carry a lot of waste!

Our bodies become overburdened with toxins. We are naturally made to eliminate and detox daily but unfortunately there are just too many toxins around us today for our body to cope. Our bodies need a little helping hand.

It is impossible to be healthy and beautiful in a body filled with toxins.

What Detoxing/Cleansing Does:

1. Removes toxins from the body

Long-term exposure to toxins (environmental pollutants, cancer-causing chemicals, preservatives, pesticides, heavy metals, and industrial waste) affects our metabolism, behaviour, immune system, and leads to disease. They are stored in tissues and cells throughout the body, including the brain, and without a detox/cleanse they can stay there for years.

2. Prevents chronic disease

Environmental toxins are responsible for many cancers, neurological diseases, heart disease, strokes etc. Our bodies do have a built-in detox function to deal with these dangers (liver, kidneys etc.) however, those systems are constantly overloaded. They can't handle the amount of daily toxins we are polluting ourselves with.

Detoxing assists and improves what our bodies are trying to do naturally. If you have an infection or an illness, it is your body's way of saying it has been overloaded with toxins.

3. Enhances immune system function

A compromised immune system makes us vulnerable to colds and flus, affecting our quality of life and productivity. Regular detoxing helps strengthen immune system functioning and fights off infection.

4. Helps us lose weight

Toxins affect the body's natural ability to burn fat, leading to weight gain. Diabetes, heart disease, and high blood pressure are directly linked to weight issues. Detoxing/Cleansing rids the body of toxins stored in fat cells (think cellulite) and increases metabolism. Toxins affect the body's natural ability to burn fat, leading to weight gain.

5. Slows premature aging

Detoxing rids the body of free radicals and heavy metals partially responsible for aging. It also helps to increase nutrient absorption, including antioxidants and vitamins that help fight oxidative stress.

6. Improves quality of life

Our bodies don't function very well when they're loaded with toxins. We may have joint pain, headaches, digestive disorders, sleep problems, and lack of energy. Depression may be eased and memory may be improved as a result of detoxification also.

7. Increases energy

You will have more mental, physical, and emotional energy after detoxing. People tend to sleep better and need less of it.

8. Improves skin health

Diet and environmental toxins affect skin. Detoxing/Cleansing improves acne, strengthens hair and nails, and gives us a natural, healthy glow.

9. Improves mental and emotional clarity

When the body's systems are aligned, a shift also occurs with our mental and emotional states. We can deal with more when we're clear and grounded. We can make better decisions, analyse accurately, and see things differently.

10. Restores balance to our body's systems

Our digestive, nervous, and hormonal systems were designed to work together to achieve optimum health and beauty. This is what our bodies want to do! When we overload them with toxins and unhealthy foods, these systems don't work as well as they should and we get sick and age faster.

Detoxing/Cleansing brings balance back and helps our systems function properly again.

When your cells and blood are clean and detoxified, your body will be able to function optimally and you can fully absorb all of the nutrients and minerals from your food. Your skin will become smoother and more radiant. Your eyes will begin to glow and lose their dark circles and puffiness, your hair and nails will begin to grow more lustrous and shiny and you will even begin to lose weight.

BUT BE AWARE – YOU MAY GET WORSE BEFORE YOU GET BETTER! You might smell bad, break out in spots, feel weak, tired, have headaches, get congested, have diarrhoea, feel nauseous, you may fill up with mucus, your nose could run, your kidneys may hurt and you might even get cold and flu-like symptoms. You will most probably want to curl up in bed and just stay there. You may even look terrible **but remember this is only temporary**. Just know your body is cleansing and letting everything out. Years of sugary drinks, dairy, processed meals, gluten etc. do not get flushed out of your cells overnight. Your body is doing some SERIOUS cleaning!

Not everybody has the strength to keep going when they embark on a cleanse. It's easier to return back to old habits when the headaches start to kick in, exhaustion takes over your body and you look worse than you did before the cleanse.

It takes a lot of will power to keep going BUT DON'T GIVE UP! Think of how you will look and feel at the end of this. Amazing, glowing, energised, radiant, full of life, happy, alert, confident and so much more. It's worth the discomfort for a few weeks. YOU CAN DO THIS! Stay strong.

How To Detox:

1. Consume only fresh raw juices and food. Organic is always best and GREEN juice.
2. Try to use only non-toxic soap, shampoo, makeup, toothpaste, cleansers etc. Essential oils are a good choice (see more in the Essential Oils chapter).
3. Exercise to get the blood to move the toxins along. Regular exercise encourages circulation in the blood and lymph system. Doing so will also enhance digestion, reduce tension, lubricate joints, and strengthen your body. People who exercise regularly have fewer toxins in their systems. All detoxification occurs first and foremost via the lymph. Our bodies contain more lymph than blood; therefore it is very important we move it and daily.
4. Get massages to help release the toxins all over your body and move it along through your lymph system.
5. Dry brush your skin (learn more about this technique in the Dry Brushing chapter).

6. Take saunas to get the toxins to come out of your skin. Infrared saunas are known to be more beneficial to the body as the infrared heat can help draw heavy metals and toxins out of your fat cells. An infrared sauna may help to accelerate detoxification.

7. Eat plenty of fibre, including brown rice and organically grown fresh fruits and vegetables. Beetroot, radishes, artichokes, cabbage, broccoli, spirulina, chlorella, grapefruit, aloe vera, apple cider vinegar, and seaweed are excellent cleansing foods.

8. Cleanse and protect the liver by taking herbs such as dandelion root, burdock, and milk thistle, and drinking green tea.

9. Take vitamin C. This helps the body produce glutathione, a liver compound that drives away toxins. Eating cruciferous vegetables and dark leafy greens also help with glutathione production too.

10. Drink at least 3 litres of water a day. Optional add fresh lemon for extra cleansing benefits.

11. Breathe deeply to allow oxygen to circulate more completely through your system.

12. Practice hydrotherapy by taking a very hot shower for 5 minutes. Follow with cold water for 30 seconds.

13. Bathe in an Epsom salt bath. The salt draws toxins from the body by making you sweat them from your skin (great to help reduce cellulite and heal acne). These natural salts are also known to help cleanse your colon when added to water. They work as a laxative, drawing water into the bowel to soften stools. These MUST be food grade. Best to take before breakfast in a powder form mixed with water. See chapter on Cellulite for a detoxing bath recipe.

14. Get rid of ANYTHING in your life that's toxic. This includes negative people, thoughts, past issues etc. LET IT ALL GO! Do some serious soul spring cleaning! Distance yourself from anything that brings you down or doesn't support your well-being.

15. Lighten up your toxin load. Eliminate alcohol, coffee, cigarettes, refined sugars, saturated fats, and even toxic

beauty products. These all act as toxins in the body and are obstacles to your healing process.

16. Remove dairy. It clogs up your lymphatic system and causes mucus throughout the body.

17. Remove processed grains. Most today are genetically modified (GMO) leading to inflammation.

18. Take away animal products (meat, eggs). These are known to cause inflammation in the body and also block up the colon.

19. Another hindrance to good health and beauty is stress. It triggers your body to release stress hormones (cortisol) into your system. In large amounts they create toxins and slow down detoxification. If you are constantly stressed, this will also lead to adrenal exhaustion. Take up yoga and meditation or any other forms of exercise to relieve stress by resetting your physical and mental reactions to the inevitable stress life will bring. Try to keep a positive mind-set. Also take adaptogenic herbs to help balance stress *(see chapter on Foods to Eat for Health and Beauty)*.

20. Have a colonic. It's a great way to get rid of bad food, bacteria, and parasites, anything that is lodged in your colon. If your colon is not clean, then the rubbish will stay there for years and eventually make you sicker and sicker as the years go by. Your colon must be clean for good health and beauty. Our colon is the sewer system of the body. When we clean the colon, we start to clean the rest of the organs too. Everything is linked. After a good cleansing take probiotics to replace any of the good bacteria that may have been washed out.

21. Fast. Fasting can heal anything. It gives your digestive system a rest and this gives the body a chance to clean. Just take in water and let the toxins leave your body. Fasting cleans out your cells, helping you to feel so much lighter and research has proven it can even heal your gut. We should fast for 15–17 hours without any food on a monthly basis. Drink loads of water during this time. Another way to fast would be to do a juice cleanse for a day or two. Intermittent fasting is another easy way to fast. This requires a 12–15 hour gap before

your next meal, for example eat your last meal at 6 pm and then don't eat anything again until 6 am the next day. This will give the body a chance to rest and rejuvenate.

22. Go to bed early and try to rise early. We should be getting in a good 7–8 hours of sleep per night. Not enough sleep can also lead to weight gain and hormonal issues. Sleep is a time where your body is repairing and healing. It plays a CRUCIAL part in detoxification.

Don't Forget!

Water is any easy way to clean out those pipes.

Drink MORE WATER.

On-going cleansing is essential to reach our highest level of health and beauty. If we do not continue to cleanse ourselves regularly, we can drive toxins deeper into the body, into the lymphatic system, which will eventually steal our health and beauty.

AND DO NOT SKIP FRUIT!!!!! Fruit is the most life-enhancing food we can put into our bodies. It is FULL of water and supplies us with all vital amino acids, minerals, vitamins and fatty acids. It supplies us with immediate energy and is one of the strongest cleansers for the body. Fruit dissolves toxic substances and cleanses our tissues and system. Every time you put a piece of fruit into your body you are putting sunshine into your cells and colours into your skin to illuminate and radiate. Fruit is what makes you beautiful. However, this can only be achieved when you clean your body out of BAD BACTERIA. Bad bacteria may feed of the fruit and cause fermentation – get those probiotics in!

Also NEVER eat fruit after a meal as this also causes fermentation, which causes excess gas and bloating. This leads to digestive issues. Fruit should always be eaten alone 30 minutes BEFORE a meal or as a snack.

Fruit contains bioelectric principles that give the electric sparks to life. – Paul C. Bragg.

I want you to remember this:

> **FRUIT IS NEEDED TO CLEAN THE BODY and GREENS ARE WHAT BUILD THE BODY.**

For a healthy, glowing, strong body we need a combination of fruits, greens, vegetables, nuts, seeds, pulses and water.

Chapter 15
Cellulite

I couldn't not talk about cellulite; it's every woman's dislike.

Most women have some sort of cellulite somewhere on their body, even skinny people.

Cellulite forms in areas with the least circulation. The puckering of skin happens when the layer of fat beneath the skin pushes against connective tissue and bulges, causing the characteristic orange-peel or cottage cheese appearance.

Women have a higher risk of developing cellulite, as there is a significant difference in the way their connective tissue and fat cells are arranged compared to men. Fat cells in women tend to be arranged vertically under the skin whereas fat cells in men are arranged horizontally and lay flat against each other.

There are a number of factors that can contribute to cellulite; it could be genetic or hormonal, maybe lack of exercise or it could just be that your body is full of toxins from years of abuse with bad dietary choices.

The primary cause of problem skin, fat, aging, poor muscle quality, cellulite, is a toxic body. It is toxins stored in the tissues and intestines. You must cleanse out your system to remove years of congestion to get you back to radiance and great health.

Cellulite is not harmful, most of us just don't like how it looks, however, if you do have copious amounts of cellulite this may be a huge warning sign that you really need to clean up your act!

If you want to cut cellulite fast, eat only grapefruits for 3 days or drink its juice. Grapefruits contain Bromelain, the same as pineapple, which is a skin cleansing enzyme, helping to break down cellulite and excess fat. Dry skin brushing is another great way to help shift things along; I will talk about that later. Most importantly we need to be moving the lymphatic system.

Cellulite Recipe:

- 2 red grapefruits
- 1 orange
- 1 handful of mint – send through juicer.

Drinking enough water daily and exercising will also help move that stubborn cellulite along. Many women who have cellulite are simply dehydrated. Good hydration may help your body cleanse itself of toxins and reduce the appearance of cellulite.

Most importantly, don't obsess over getting rid of it. It took years to get there so it won't disappear overnight and may never completely disappear. Women's bodies store fat, we have to accept that. Love yourself as you are.

Detox Bath For Cellulite:

- ¼ cup Epsom salts
- ¼ cup baking soda
- 10 drops of an essential oil such as cypress, geranium or grapefruit.
- Relax and enjoy.

Epsom salts are known to move the lymphatic system and help to draw toxins out of the body.

> **Sickness is the result of the retention of waste in the body – Dr Norman Walker.**

Eat Foods To Beat Cellulite:

1. Grapefruit
2. Apple Cider Vinegar
3. Coconut oil
4. Chlorella
5. Essential Fatty Acids – Omega-3
6. Avocados
7. Pineapple
8. Citrus fruits
9. Cacao / Raw Chocolate
10. Drink water.

Essential Oils For Cellulite:

1. Cypress
2. Grapefruit
3. Lemon
4. Juniper Berry
5. Lime

Use with a carrier oil such as coconut oil and apply daily to problem areas to boost your lymphatic system.
Also try these yoga poses:

1. Eagle
2. Bridge
3. Plough
4. Chair
5. Twisted lunge
6. Reverse plank / table top
7. Shoulder stand.

Chapter 16
Dry Skin Brushing for Beauty and Health

Our skin is constantly eliminating waste products but if your skin is overrun with toxins or dead skin cells, it will not be able to eliminate wastes from your body efficiently and this is one reason why we have that nasty cellulite.

Skin brushing daily is wonderful for circulation, toning, cleansing and healing. It helps to purify lymph so it's able to detoxify your blood and tissues. It removes old skin cells, uric acid crystals and toxic waste that come up through the skins pores.

Here are 7 reasons why you need to start brushing today:

1. **It stimulates your lymphatic system** In your body, your lymphatic system is the system responsible for eliminating cellular waste products. When your lymphatic system is not working properly, waste and toxins can build up and make you sick and less than beautiful. Lymphatic congestion is a major factor leading to inflammation and disease. By stimulating your lymphatic system and helping it release toxins, dry skin brushing is a powerful detoxification aid. Our bodies contain more lymph than blood so it is vital we move it.

2. **Exfoliation** Dry skin brushing removes dead dry skin, improving appearance, clearing your clogged pores, and allowing your skin to 'breathe'.

3. **Increases circulation** When you dry brush, it increases circulation to your skin, which encourages the elimination of metabolic waste. It is also known to help your face glow but don't use the brush on your face.
4. **Reduces cellulite** We all want rid of this, right ladies? We all hate it. Well dry skin brushing is said to help reduce cellulite by removing toxins that may break down connective tissue. It helps to exfoliate the skin, smoothing out little lumps and bumps.
5. **Stress relief** The act of dry brushing has been described as meditative and may reduce muscle tension, calming your mind, and relieving stress.
6. **Improves digestion and kidney function** Dry skin brushing may go even deeper, helping to support your digestion and organ function.
7. **It feels amazing!** It gives you glowing and tighter skin, who doesn't want this?

Dry Brushing – How to Do It:

First, you'll need a high-quality dry brush. Look for ones with bristles made from natural materials. Ideally, choose a brush with a long handle so you can reach your entire back and other hard-to-reach spots.

Dry skin brushing should be done daily for best results if you are suffering from a lot of cellulite. Try incorporating it into your normal daily routine, such as doing your brushing before a morning shower. It should always be done on dry skin and will only take 5 minutes.

When brushing, always brush toward your heart, this is best for circulation and your lymphatic system. You can brush your entire body (including the soles of your feet). Start at your feet and work your way up your legs to your arms, chest, back, and stomach. Avoid brushing your face (*unless you have a special brush designed for this delicate skin*), your genitals, breasts, nipples or any areas with irritations or abrasions (*including varicose veins*). Pay attention to the inner thigh and under arms; these are hot spots for removing toxins. You can also add a little coconut oil to the brush or an essential oil. Try to wash your brush once a week.

As soon as you have finished dry brushing take a shower, then dry off your body and finally massage into your skin, organic cold pressed coconut oil with a few drops of a detoxing essential oil such as lemon or grapefruit.

Happy Brushing!

Chapter 17
The Link Between Acne and Gut Health

Acne is painful, (so, so painful, I KNOW!) and not only that it looks ugly!

Acne is a distress signal that is related to diet, stress, a lack of beneficial bacteria in the gut and on the skin, a fluctuation of hormone levels, and an accumulation of toxic materials somewhere in the body.

The most common treatments for acne are quick-fix solutions to kill the bacteria as fast as possible. Sometimes we even resort to highly toxic pharmaceutical medications, like I did.

These treatments dry out the skin and don't really do much for you. Harsh, medicated soaps and ointments or even toxic pharmaceuticals do not get to the root cause of the problem. Therefore, the acne either returns or stays put! These treatments can even damage the skin. I have been left with permanent acne scarring.

The root cause of your acne is often related to inflammation. Inflammation always begins in the gut. Inflammation then expresses itself on the outside, through our skin. The skin reddens, swells, and sometimes fills with fluid or waxy sebum.

The conventional wisdom is that acne develops when sebaceous (oil) glands; attached to hair follicles are stimulated during puberty by elevated levels of male hormones (testosterone). This increased oil production starts a cascade of events that result in inflammation. However, I believe gut dysbiosis and increased intestinal permeability (aka leaky gut) are also one of the root causes of acne and when acne appears, the underlying gut issues might have been present for some time.

Even sometimes from birth. When there's an increased sebum production associated with hormones, the low-grade inflammation caused by leaky gut and gut dysbiosis often manifests itself as acne. Research has now found that there are certain probiotic strains that can control excess sebum production. Having enough beneficial bacterial strains in your gut is VERY important when dealing with ANY skin condition. All the creams and lotions you apply to your skin will not work; you have to correct what is going wrong on the inside first.

Diet is also a very critical factor in the quest for beautiful skin. As I mentioned earlier not once did my doctor or dermatologist ask me what I was eating or drinking. Food plays a HUGE role in your skin health too. Foods that frequently contribute to inflammation are: gluten, dairy, hydrogenated oils and sugar. When I was suffering with severe acne my dairy and gluten intake was really high. I was eating and drinking dairy and bread at every single meal and even as snacks. Research has proven that dairy is one of the biggest causes of acne. There are a few reasons why this happens, one is down to the amount of hormones in dairy, which mess with our hormones and the other reason is because the protein, casein has been shown to trigger immune responses, which raises inflammation. When the body is inflamed we get bad skin and this may also lead to intestinal permeability (leaky gut). To achieve beautiful skin you MUST remove dairy. Sugar is also a BIG factor as it raises insulin levels, which may increase hormones that stimulate sebum to over produce. Sugar also causes inflammation and feeds the bad bacteria in our guts. PLUS it ages us rapidly.

In order to heal acne, we MUST increase our intake of good bacteria (probiotics) because they:

- Help to break down food.
- Reduce inflammation.
- Heal and repair the lining of the intestinal wall.
- Help to transform and shuttle out toxins from the body.
- Keep yeast overgrowth and pathogenic microbes in check.
- They control excess sebum production.
- They balance hormones.

- Certain strains can control how we deal with stress.
- They promote glowing skin.
- They crowd out the bad bacteria.

> **Beautiful skin begins with the healthy population of good bacteria.**

Skin glows with a probiotic-rich diet. Scars soften and disappear. Breakouts happen less frequently, if at all.

> **IF YOU ARE SUFFERING FROM ACNE, REMEMBER IT IS OFTEN RELATED TO INFLAMMATION AND ALL INFLAMMATION BEGINS IN THE GUT.**

The combination of probiotics and a change in diet is needed for ALL skin disorders.

Another very important factor when dealing with a skin problem is to avoid synthetic, toxic beauty products as these too can cause your skin to flare up. I made that mistake in my acne days and I have now been left with scars. See chapter on Essential Oils and how you can make your skin more beautiful from the outside in too. Most commercial beauty products today are packed full of chemicals, which are VERY damaging to our skin. If you start to use essential oils and carrier oils, you can heal your skin and prevent scarring. Something I wish I had known back then.

As always I will recommend that you also start juicing green vegetables too. This is a remedy that works like magic for me. It makes my skin glow from the inside out and as an added bonus they slow aging down too.

If you are suffering from any other skin issue, for example, rosacea, eczema etc. usually what treatments work for acne works for them too. They all root from the same thing and that is INFLAMMATION.

Acne Tips:

- Reduce your intake of sugar, dairy and gluten.
- Remove industrial seed oils from your diet. They contribute to inflammation and make acne worse, e.g. corn oil, rapeseed oils, hydrogenated oils, trans fats, etc. These are also in processed foods and takeaways.
- Take good bacteria (probiotics/fermented foods). These are good for your health and significantly reduce the occurrence of acne and other skin problems, making the skin more beautiful from the outside in. Probiotics are a MUST for clear skin. They reduce inflammation in the gut and they balance hormones.
- Drink more water. Also adding lemon to your water will encourage beautiful, glowing skin.
- Limit stress. Stress disrupts the ratio of good and bad bacteria in the gut, which also leads to breakouts.
- Use essential oils and carrier oils on the skin; see Essential Oils chapter for more on this. Avoid toxic commercial beauty products as much as you can, these can aggravate the situation.
- Take in adaptogenic herbs such as schizandra berry and holy basil/tulsi.
- Beauty is an inside job. You HAVE to get to the root cause of why you have the skin disorder. One important thing to remember EVERYTHING is caused by inflammation. If you take antibiotics for acne or any skin condition, it will not go away and you will have also wiped out ALL of your good gut bacteria, which as you know now is ESSENTIAL for beautiful skin.

I used to suffer terribly with body acne on my shoulders, back etc. you may want to also have a healing bath once or twice a week using 1 tbsp. coconut oil and 2-5 drops of the essential oil neem.

Chapter 18
Sugar

> **Sugar is poison.**

Sugar will rip holes in your intestinal lining and will also cause leaky gut syndrome. It feeds the growth of yeast, candida and bad bacteria, which will further damage your gut. It eats away at your intestinal wall.

Sugar is the fastest thing that will age you.

Sugar is found in almost EVERYTHING! From breakfast cereals, ketchups, salad dressings, bread, yoghurts, you name it, it's there. Sugar is made from refined sugarcane and sugar beets, in a process that creates those white crystals we know. This sugar is killing us.

Sugar demineralizes your body, pulls calcium from your bones, causing osteoporosis, damages your immune system, leads to heart disease, high blood pressure, diabetes, arthritis, messes up your hormones, clogs up your arteries and leads to clots. It feeds disease! Bacteria, parasites, mold, yeast and cancer cells thrive off it. It causes inflammation in EVERY cell in your body, which also leads to premature aging and skin problems like acne, psoriasis and rosacea. STAY AWAY!

Sugar also makes you FAT.

Refined sugar is a drug that causes mood swings, depression, inflammation and so much more. Research is now linking sugar to Type 3 diabetes known as Alzheimer's.

Also stay away from artificial sweeteners. They are toxic and seriously dangerous to your health. They are now linking sweeteners such as Splenda to cancers and even brain damage. Plus they alter your microbiome; they feed the bad bacteria in your gut. Artificial sweeteners also cause weight problems as they may make you more susceptible to overeating and can trigger insulin to be released. This increases fat storage. Not good news if you are trying to lose weight.

Watch Out For These:

- Chewing gum
- Soft drinks
- Salad dressings
- Yoghurts
- Breakfast cereals
- Children's chewable vitamins / adult vitamins
- Processed foods
- 'DIET' food and drinks
- Read the labels of everything you buy. Watch out for sugar hidden under names such as maltodextrin, maltose, sucrose, high-fructose corn syrup, molasses, dextrose, rice syrup, barley malt, dextrose, sucralose, saccharin, aspartame and more. I told you it's everywhere.

AND STAY AWAY FROM AGAVE! It is NOT healthy and is extremely aging!

- Agave is in every health food store and almost every health food alternative. It is deemed as the new 'healthy' alternative to sugar, which everyone is using in their raw food bars, smoothies, drinks, raw desserts and any other health food recipes promoted today. STAY AWAY from it! It is highly processed and has a fructose content of up to 90%. Agave is almost all fructose (a highly processed sugar). Fructose is extremely bad for your health. Studies have shown that it can cause cancer, obesity, cause inflammation in the body and damages the liver, as well as various other chronic conditions.

- Agave syrup or agave nectar is not a whole food found in nature. It has undergone extensive processing to make it into this liquid form.
- The best sweetener is stevia. Raw honey is even better as it is full of antioxidants, vitamins and minerals and also has amazing beauty and healing properties. Another alternative is maple syrup. It is healthier than agave but still must only be used in small quantities.

When we eat sugar in any shape or form, in food, in sweets, in liquid, it ferments in the body causing the formation of acetic acid. Acetic acid is a powerful destructive acid that has been used to burn warts off the skin. Imagine what it does to your intestines.

Sugar is a dead processed product. The only sugars that are of any value to the human body are the natural sugars found in raw fruits and honey. Fruit is a healer to our body, never think of a fruit as a processed sugar. We need fruit!

Chapter 19
SOY

GMO Soy is NOT healthy and it can cause severe health problems.

Soybeans contain phytoestrogens, which mimic the body's natural oestrogen hormones. For men, this can lead to testosterone imbalance, infertility, low sperm count, and increased risk of cancers such as prostate. For women, it may cause oestrogen dominance, which has been linked to infertility, and menstrual troubles. It causes abdominal stress and pancreatic problems including cancer.

These phytoestrogens are so strong that a baby consuming only soy formula is consuming the equivalent hormones of 4 birth control pills a day! I was shocked to see they are now selling soy milk for children in the supermarkets. Please do not buy this.

The high levels of phytic acid in soy also inhibit the body's ability to absorb important minerals, including zinc, calcium, copper, iron and magnesium, which many people are dangerously deficient in today.

Soy also contains protease inhibitors, which can block the enzymes that are necessary for the digestion of certain proteins.

The goitrogens in soy are potent anti-thyroid compounds that can lead to endocrine disruption and thyroid disorders. As we now know, the thyroid controls the metabolism, among other very important functions in the body, and slowing it down will lead to weight gain and further problems. Infants on soy formula also have a much higher risk of autoimmune thyroid disease.

Soy is often promoted as an alternative food for celiac and gluten intolerant people, but its lectins can be harmful to the intestines and prevent healing even when gluten is removed. Soy may also be another culprit to bring on leaky gut.

Consumption of soy foods increases the body's need for vitamin D, vitamin B12, calcium and magnesium.

Animals who are fed soy can suffer many of the same health consequences as people who consume too much soy, and these harmful properties are then passed on in their meat, which of course then goes into our system when we eat the meat.

Soy is also heavily contaminated with pesticides. These pesticides cause damage to our nervous system, reproductive system, our hormones and they can even cause behavioural abnormalities. Most of today's soy is all GMO'd *(genetically modified)*. Anything that is GMO'd will not be recognised by the human body. This will cause inflammation.

Soy is not natural. It is toxic and we should not be consuming it.

What About Asian Countries Where Soy Is Consumed In Large Amounts?

People in these countries do not consume as much soy as we assume they do. In fact, in most places, soy-based foods are served as a condiment, not a main course and not as a replacement for animal protein. In addition, these foods are fermented or traditionally prepared, which is better for our health.

Fermented Soy

If you are going to consume soy, it is least harmful in its fermented state. Foods like tempeh and miso have some fantastic health promoting properties and many of the harmful anti-nutrients are fermented out. Just look for ones that have been traditionally fermented. Edamame may also be enjoyed in moderation as they contain fewer toxins. Moderation is the key word with soy, don't go crazy.

Watch out – Soy Is EVERYWHERE!

Almost all processed foods contain some form of soy. Check the foods you buy for these ingredients: soy lecithin, soy protein concentrate, soy protein isolate, texturized vegetable protein, hydrolysed vegetable protein or any other phrase containing the word 'SOY'.

Just avoid anything with soy in it, even traces of soy.

Chapter 20
Dairy and the GUT

If I had one wish for everyone, it would be to STOP consuming dairy. Nobody should be eating or drinking it. We are not baby cows!

I used to live on dairy. I drank pints of milk; milk for me was my water. I loved yoghurts and cheese; I drowned my cereal in milk and guess what? I also suffered badly from acne. Research has proven that dairy is one of the causes of this horrible skin condition. We've already talked about the gut connection with acne but now I want to go into dairy a little deeper because I encourage everyone to reduce their intake and slowly take it out of their diet for good.

We have always believed that dairy is something humans should consume in order for us to have strong bones and prevent us from developing osteoporosis later on in life, but this a load of rubbish. It shouldn't be in our diet. The natural purpose of cow's milk is to feed baby cows. When the baby grows up, they too, stop drinking milk and shift to eating grass. It is only we humans who continue to consume milk after weaning but not from our own mothers – we drink milk from other animals. No adult cows ever drink milk, and adult humans are certainly not meant to be drinking it either!

The chemical consumption of cow's milk is different from that of human milk, and therefore are bodies are not designed to break it down.

The main protein in cow's milk is called casein and the other protein is whey. The molecules of casein are too huge for humans to digest. Without the necessary enzymes such as lactase to break it down, casein coagulates in our stomach and is very difficult for our bodies to break down. Casein is such a strong binder that it has also been used as an ingredient in wood glue. As I mentioned earlier, casein has a similar effect to gluten, which damages and inflames the small intestine leading to the development of leaky gut. Whey is the other problem here because this causes insulin to be released; when this happens it may trigger skin issues like acne. Do you ever see body builders with acne all over their shoulders? This is a reason why. Research has also found dairy to be another cause of autoimmune diseases.

Once dairy is put into our bodies, it becomes extremely acid-forming. Anything acid forming depletes beauty and encourages weight gain as well as inflammation. But dairy has another downside: **MUCUS.**

Mucus is clear and slippery and coats anything we ingest. Excessive mucus can begin to harden and build up along the walls of our intestines, adding to sludge and slowing down matter moving through the intestinal tract. If your colon gets blocked or backed up, toxins leak into the bloodstream, which then causes inflammation. Dairy is one of the most mucus-forming foods there is. Remember this: Think of glue when you see dairy.

Dairy products begin to wreak havoc on our bodies as soon as they are ingested, so our bodies then try to desperately get rid of them in different ways such as phlegm, mucus or spots.

In addition to creating mucus, conventional dairy is packed with hormones, pesticides, antibiotics and drugs. These drugs inevitably end up in our milk and make their way into our system.

Milk and cheese are among the top causes of arthritis, constipation, allergies, IBS, PCOS, fibromyalgia, endometriosis, obesity, lung problems, anaemia, ovarian problems, eczema, skin rashes, acne, cancer and more. Research is now suggesting that dairy also feeds cancer cells.

Milk has one purpose, to make living things grow. Why as adults are we still consuming it?

Calcium and Osteoporosis

I want you to remember – milk does NOT put calcium in our bones. Cow's milk does have a lot of calcium in it but much of it is not assimilated or used by the human body. It is also highly acidic when ingested and the increased acid load in the body causes us to lose calcium from our bones, therefore, the more dairy we take the more chance we have of developing bone issues.

The best sources for calcium are dark leafy greens, green vegetables as well as sea vegetables and nuts and seeds. They are high in calcium, magnesium and vitamin K and are highly alkaline. These minerals and vitamins combined are what give us strong bones, NOT just calcium. We also need vitamin D too. This is a key note to remember, you MUST have magnesium and calcium together. It's actually magnesium with vitamin D, (sunshine) and vitamin K, (greens) that gives us strong bones more so than the calcium. When it comes to promoting strong bones in children, encouraging them to play sports is wiser than telling them to drink copious amounts of milk – exercise helps to build strong bones and they should also be outside getting vitamin D.

"Nothing clogs up your intestines faster than cheese and dairy. You might as well be swallowing glue."
– Markus Rothkranz

People are terrified today to skip out the dairy from their diet because we have been programmed and brain-washed from birth to believe from advertising that if we do not eat dairy we will not have strong bones and will later develop osteoporosis. This is hugely a load of crap! Change your mind-set please! Where do you think a cow gets its big muscles from? Or all the vegan animals out there, such as gorillas, hippos, elephants etc. They do not eat meat or dairy and look how strong and muscular they are. THEY EAT GREENS!!! Greens are where the amino acids are that our bodies need to develop strong muscles and are also LOADED with calcium, magnesium and vitamin K.

If you really do not want to give up dairy, then I suggest you try some alternatives such as; goat's milk and goat's cheese. We digest goat's milk better than cow's milk. Sheep's milk and sheep's cheese is the next best choice.

If you suffer from any digestive issues; autoimmune disease; weight gain; type 2 diabetes; PMS; infertility; skin disorders like acne, rosacea, eczema or ANY chronic disease, you MUST stay away from ALL dairy. The root cause of ALL is inflammation. Dairy triggers inflammation.

GREENS HAVE MORE NUTRITION THAN ALMOST ANYTHING ON THE PLANET. EAT MORE GREENS!

Good Sources Of Plant Based Calcium Include:

• Bok choy	• Spinach
• Broccoli	• Cucumber
• Cauliflower	• Sea Vegetables
• Chlorella	• Turnip Greens
• Kale	• Beet Greens
• Sesame Seeds	• Collard Greens
• Swiss Chard	• Spirulina
• Romaine Lettuce	• Moringa
• **ALL** dark leafy greens	• Nuts and seeds
	• Tahini

Chapter 21
BREAD and GLUTEN on the Gut

"Bread is highly mucus-forming in the body. It's addictive and aging." – Markus Rothkranz

As we mentioned earlier, gluten causes holes in the intestinal lining and is responsible for leaky gut. It causes severe inflammation in our gut. Bread has no nutritional value. It turns into sugar in your body. This sugar then feeds parasites, bacteria, yeast, fungus, cancer and diabetes and also leads to weight gain. Gluten is now linked to be a cause in autoimmune diseases. It is also known to damage the cartilage in joints as it causes so much inflammation. This inflammation then leads to arthritis.

Eliminating gluten can completely improve your overall health and beauty. Cutting it out will prevent sugar and carbohydrate cravings, it will help to stabilise your moods and even help you to lose weight. Research has also found that by eliminating ALL gluten from your diet conditions such as: rheumatoid arthritis, acne, dermatitis, psoriasis, ulcerative colitis etc. will improve. Results will not happen overnight as they say it can take around 3 months to get gluten out of your system completely; however, over time you will start to see a difference, just don't give up! I used to be a bread addict and couldn't lose weight or feel like I could get off the stuff. If I can do it, so can YOU!

YOU CANNOT BUILD HEALTHY CELLS FROM BREAD, CEREALS AND PASTAS.

Most people are gluten intolerant because we shouldn't be eating as much as we are today.

> **"THE MOST SEVERE KIND OF GLUTEN INTOLEARNCE IS DEPRESSION."**
> **– Patrick Holford**

Depression is also linked to the gut as it is caused by inflammation and when the gut is inflamed the brain is inflamed and on FIRE! If you suffer from lack of concentration, depression, insomnia, anxiety etc. look into your gut. Chances are its leaking. We've already talked about the vagus nerve. The vagus nerve runs from your gut to your brain and they are in constant communication all day long.

Wheat today has too much gluten and has been extremely modified so the manufacturers can sell more and make more money. Gluten is a family of proteins found in many grains. It is what makes dough doughy and bread airy. No humans can digest it completely. We do not have the enzymes to fully digest the proteins. The gluten content in foods today has grown rapidly over the years and it is causing severe inflammation in the gut. The bread we consume today is not what our grandparents used to eat. It has all been sprayed with pesticides that are causing cancer and intestinal permeability (leaky gut) and the wheat has been hybridized through natural breeding techniques. The body cannot recognise it as a food anymore because it has been so messed with. My advice is to stay away from it as much as you can. It is destroying your beauty and your gut.

Watch out though gluten is also hidden EVERYWHERE!

Medications, spices, toothpastes, additives and even in your make-up! It's a hard one to stay away from.

> **Gluten is foreign to our body.**

Chapter 22
Medications and Painkillers

As I mentioned earlier, I spent a good deal of my teenage years on antibiotics to try to cure my acne not knowing it was also destroying my gut.

Antibiotics are designed to kill ALL bacteria. They are grenades to the gut. They wipe out EVERYTHING! This leads to a growth in bad bacteria, destroying your gut and increasing intestinal permeability. Stay away from them, unless you really need to take them as an emergency, and if you do make sure you load up on probiotics.

Painkillers also irritate the gut. If used regularly, they can lead to future problems such as arthritis, inflammation and once again leaky gut. Painkillers do not do anything for you except stop the pain. That pain is there for a reason, it is telling you something is wrong. When you cover it over with a painkiller whatever is wrong is still happening, you now just can't feel it. You need to address the pain and heal it, not mask it over. Take anti-inflammatory foods such as turmeric, ginger, cayenne pepper, olives, chia seeds etc. These will all help to heal you. Medications also mask over our problems. They DO NOT get to the root cause of the condition and THEY WILL NOT heal you. Over time they also lead to more inflammation in the body, which will then cause further dis-ease.

Chapter 23
PCOS

I want to mention PCOS briefly as new research is also starting to bring to light that this too may be caused by a leaky gut.

Polycystic ovary syndrome is a problem in which a woman's hormones are out of balance. It can cause problems with your periods and make it difficult to get pregnant. PCOS may also cause unwanted changes in the way you look, for example facial hair and acne. If it isn't treated, over time, it can lead to serious health problems, such as diabetes and heart disease.

Most women with PCOS grow many small cysts on their ovaries. That is why it is called polycystic ovary syndrome. The cysts are not harmful but lead to hormone imbalances.

In PCOS, the sex hormones (testosterone and progesterone) get out of balance. One hormone change triggers another, which changes another. Normally, the ovaries make a tiny amount of male sex hormones (androgens). In PCOS, they start making slightly more androgens. This may cause you to stop ovulating, get acne, and grow extra facial and body hair. With PCOS you may also be oestrogen dominant. You need to consume adaptogenic herbs to balance your hormones such as holy basil and ashwagandha.

The body may have a problem using insulin, called insulin resistance. When the body doesn't use insulin well, blood sugar levels go up. Over time, this increases your chance of getting diabetes.

Rather than masking this with antibiotics, or the hormonal contraceptive, get empowered, and use food as a tool for change.

Eat More Of These Foods To Fight PCOS Naturally:

Romaine lettuce	Turnip greens	Cinnamon	Crimini mushrooms
Broccoli	Salmon	Kale	Sesame seeds
Pumpkin seeds	Chia seeds	Almonds	Apple cider vinegar
Raw cacao powder	Spinach	Avocado	Eat or drink more greens
Holy Basil / Tulsi	Ashwagandha	Hemp seeds	Maca
Take in more healthy fats (omega-3)	**Probiotics are a MUST and Fermented foods.**		

Foods to Avoid For PCOS (Same As For Leaky Gut):

Sugar	Dairy	Red meat	All white flour products
Gluten	Soy	Artificial sweeteners	Processed foods
Hydrogenated oils, trans fats etc.			
Maintaining a healthy gut microbiome is CRITICAL to PCOS health.			

Dairy and sugar are one of the biggest factors and root causes of PCOS. If you are suffering from PCOS, it is a MUST you remove ALL dairy from your diet. A typical dairy cow is kept pregnant and/or lactating for most of the year. This really messes up their hormones, and those hormones wind up in our milk/dairy products, which then mess with our hormones. This is really not good news for PCOS sufferers or anyone with other hormonal conditions. These extra hormones from the cow are also known to be another reason why we develop bad skin conditions such as acne as previously mentioned.

Research is now also bringing to light that PCOS may be caused by a lack of good bugs in the gut. These good bugs play a role in keeping your hormones happy and balanced as well as calm down any inflammation. As with everything else, when you heal your gut, you heal so much more.

Chapter 24
The Miracle of Coconut Oil for Healing Your GUT

Everyone is going coconut crazy these days. I know I am. I use it for absolutely everything!

Coconut oil has amazing health and beauty benefits including balancing hormones, killing candida, improving digestion, helping with weight loss and even improving memory. Research has found the MCT in coconut oil can even reverse Alzheimer's. Coconut oil should be your go-to oil for everything. No-one should be without it.

The healthy saturated fats are also an integral part to healing your gut. Lauric, capric and caprylic acids in coconut oil have anti-microbial, anti-fungal and anti-viral properties. The medium-chain fatty acids in coconut oil are easy to absorb, digest, and move through the blood and into the liver to be quickly converted right into energy. The oil also inactivates the bad guys, such as candida, all while suppressing inflammation and repairing tissue to help heal the gut. The oil turns into monolaurin once it reaches your gut, which is a very powerful anti-microbial agent. It helps regulate the bad bacteria and supports the good bacteria, all while helping to reduce inflammation and leaky gut. People suffering with ulcerative colitis, Crohn's disease and other types of inflammatory bowel diseases have all benefited from the ingestion of coconut oil. It is the anti-inflammatory and healing effects of coconut oil in addition to its easy digestibility, that play a role in soothing inflammation in the digestive tract, which are characteristic of these inflammatory digestive diseases.

Coconut oil, in addition to the medium chain fatty acids, is rich in vitamin E, vitamin K and iron. It also contains compounds such as phenolic anti-oxidants that are known to help our systems in combating different health issues and it is known to strengthen your body's immune system. It's powerful stuff!

Coconut oil also stimulates your thyroid, which can help maintain your metabolism's natural rhythm. This occurs because the medium chain fatty acids present in coconut oil have the properties of raising your metabolic and basal temperature, which will promote weight loss and increase energy. These basic functions of the body are altered when your thyroid gland is not functioning properly.

I highly recommend if you are also suffering from acne to use coconut oil topically on your skin as well. I'm a huge fan of using coconut oil on my face, to remove make-up and I leave it on overnight as a deep face mask whilst I sleep. As we mentioned earlier, coconut oil is the source of 2 of the most powerful anti-microbial agents, known as capric acid and lauric acid. These help to kill any bad bacteria on the skin. Its antibiotic properties can effectively eliminate the bacteria, which cause acne. Coconut oil can also be used to heal your acne scarring when applied topically. Taking coconut oil internally also helps with acne. I like to take 1 tbsp. of coconut oil in matcha green tea with manuka honey everyday but just see what works well for you. And if you are concerned about aging, coconut oil also helps increase the elasticity of the skin. It helps to keep your skin smooth, healthy and wrinkle free. Always buy organic, cold-pressed, extra virgin. There are a lot of processed ones out there on the market, which are not good for you. Using coconut oil on your skin is a much better option than buying toxic commercial facial washes.

And don't forget the other coconut products too. ALL coconut products are good for your gut and beauty. Stock up on coconut water (fresh), coconut milk, coconut flour etc. Go crazy for anything coconut, they not only nourish the thyroid gland and keep our gut and skin healthy; they also keep ALL of our hormones in balance. Coconut is awesome!

Chapter 25
Foods That Steal Our Beauty and Health

- Dairy (all kinds of dairy) milk, yoghurt, cream, cheese, whey protein powders and casein powders.
- Sugar (brown rice syrup, barley malt syrup, sucrose, fructose, high-fructose corn syrup, maltose, maltodextrin, dextrose, evaporated cane syrup, corn syrup, malt, beet sugar, and yes even agave syrup).
- Nicotine.
- Red meat.
- Trans fats/refined oils (margarine, hydrogenated oils, soybean oil, canola oil, rapeseed oil, vegetable oil, cottonseed oil, corn oil, sunflower oil).
- Sodas.
- Fast food.
- Processed foods.
- Fried foods.
- Vinegars such as balsamic. It is acid forming and should only be consumed occasionally.
- Artificial sweeteners (e.g. Splenda, Sweet n Low etc.). These cause weight gain as they alter the bacteria in our gut, lead to inflammation and cause skin problems too.
- Alcohol.
- Lunch meats.
- Antibiotics.
- Steroids.
- Wheat/Gluten.
- Pork.

- Corn.
- White rice.
- White flour products.
- White pastas.
- Peanuts (They are high in mold).
- Decaf coffee / coffee.

Chapter 26
Juicing

The key to outstanding beauty and health I believe is JUICE! I started juicing many years ago with a goal only to lose weight that I had piled on after my diagnosis with Graves' disease. I committed to Jason Vales 7 day juice cleanse because I was desperate to lose weight. To my astonishment, I couldn't believe the extra benefits that came with it. I had never felt so well. My mind was clear, my energy was high, my skin started to glow, I woke up early with a desire to work out every day, my eyes were sparkling, I couldn't believe how amazing I felt. I had never had this before. I became addicted to that feeling of wellness and being ALIVE and I want YOU to get that feeling too.

I want you to get into the habit of drinking fresh vegetables daily. I think it is one of the fastest ways to transform your body, beauty and health.

When you drink fresh-made green juice, the vitamins, minerals and enzymes go straight into your system without having to be broken down. You are literally getting an infusion of goodness straight into your bloodstream. A cocktail of beautiful vitamins and minerals, which will help heal you and make you look and feel absolutely amazing!

I recommend that you drink your juice first thing in the morning to give you a natural energy boost without resorting to stimulants like coffee. It can revitalize your energy levels within as little as 20 minutes and this is only the beginning of its benefits. I am addicted to how good I feel after a juice. Trust me, you will love it!

Fresh juices filled with chlorophyll from green-leafy foods such as celery, parsley, spinach, kale, broccoli, Swiss chard etc.

and green fruits such as pear, cucumber and apples are a fabulous way to maintain a beautiful, strong body for a lifetime.

As mentioned earlier, most of us have impaired digestion as a result of making poor diet choices over the years. This limits your body's ability to absorb all of the nutrients from the vegetables. Juicing will help to 'pre-digest' them for you so you will receive most of the nutrition, rather than having it go down the toilet.

Juicing is also an easy way to take in more vegetables daily. We often don't eat enough of them and greens/vegetables are VERY important if you want to stay dis-ease free, glowing and ageless.

Juicing Helps With:

- Weight loss.
- Boosts immune system.
- Increases your energy.
- Supports your brain health.
- Increases libido.
- Gives more power and stamina for exercise.
- Helps with digestion problems.
- Clears skin problems like acne, psoriasis and rosacea.
- Can heal diseases and inflammation such as cancer, diabetes, arthritis etc.
- Gives you vitality and life back.
- Clears mental fog.
- Keeps you focused and alert.
- And so much more… Trust me, you will get addicted to the feeling you get from juicing!

Greens clean the body, they remove toxins; they act as a vacuum cleaner making everything shiny and new, sweeping everything out of us. If your diet is very toxic and you are eating a lot of processed meals, sugar, gluten, high fat foods etc., you need a green juice even more. If you are trying to lose weight and you're not, chances are your body is highly toxic/acidic and you need to do a good cleanse to kick start your weight loss. Juicing is perfect for this.

Juicing pushes nutrients through your blood stream and into your liver rapidly; this results in skin that is dewy and beautiful. Skin remains radiant due to the cellular cleansing – beauty begins with our cells. The benefits are enormous, including but not limited to, radiant skin, healthy hair and nails.

It is also great for kids too, if you are struggling to get fruits and vegetables into their diet. They can also enjoy on a regular basis with a meal or snack. They will love them, I promise. Kids love anything that has colour so make it bright.

I do heavily recommend that you focus on *green juice* and NOT fruit juice. This is very important because fruit contains too much sugar (fructose), and when juiced it may spike your insulin levels. Not great for diabetes or if you need to lose weight. You can add in a green apple, kiwi or berries to give your juice flavour as these are low in sugar but the bulk of it should come from organic green vegetables like spinach, celery, kale, Swiss chard etc. It may take some time to get used to the flavour, so if you are new to juicing, I suggest you add more mild-tasting vegetables like celery, spinach, romaine lettuce and then work your way up to the more bitter ones like kale, Swiss chard, fennel etc.

Also add in lemons, limes and fresh ginger.

If you are new to juicing and find that you have unusual bowel movements, such as diarrhoea after consuming a juice, don't worry, this is usually a sign you are dealing with a lot of toxins in your body. Don't give up, eventually this should stop.

Which Types Of Juicers Are Best?

High speed blenders like the Vitamix are great for green smoothies but they are not the best juicers. There are so many juicers out there, it can all be confusing but basically the slower the juice is extracted, the more nutrients are preserved. If you are new to juicing, I recommend a mid-priced juicer. You want a juicer that does not create a lot of heat. Heating destroys vitamins and enzymes, and we know how important those enzymes are for our beauty and health.

I strongly recommend using organic vegetables as much as possible, and drinking it as soon as you have made it. Vegetable juice is highly perishable so it's best to drink all of your juice immediately.

A juicer for me is a must if you want to live a healthy, vibrant, disease free life.

When you start to drink juices daily you will notice your hair, skin, nails, your thoughts; everything starts to shine. It really is my favourite thing. You may hear a lot of negative comments regarding juicing in the media and your doctor/nutritionist may even frown upon them but from my own personal experience it has done nothing but brought me amazing health and beautiful skin. This is what I want for you.

> "We should never underestimate the power of freshly extracted fruit and vegetable juices."
> – Jason Vale

Chapter 27
Green Juice and LEAKY GUT

Green juicing is so beneficial for cleansing the body and being kind to a leaky gut. Green juicing gives the digestive track a little break and promotes elimination, which helps cleanse and detoxify. Cleansing is very important for leaky gut sufferers. We need as much help as we can get since our guts leak toxins into our bodies. Green juicing helps to get the bowels moving. This moves some of those toxins out of the body. Green juices also stop inflammation, this is VERY important. Juicing is easy and it tastes so good! Candida, PCOS and acne sufferers would also benefit heaps from GREEN JUICE!

Get Juicing!
The Differences Between Juicing And Blending

I always recommend that you juice and blend. They are both amazing for you. A juicer will extract the juice only and remove the pulp from the fruit and vegetables. The fibre has been taken away. While the fibre is very important for proper bowel function, it is actually the juice that nourishes us. When you drink the juice it goes straight into your veins, your blood and misses the digestion stage. If you have any health issues, this is extremely important. Digestion is where we tend to lose all of the vital nutrients that our body needs. The juicer in effect digests the food for you. With juice, you are guaranteed to get all of the necessary vitamins and minerals from the fruits and vegetables. With blending there is no guarantee that you will receive all of the nutrition because it still has to be digested. If you are looking for true health and vitality, juicing is what you need to do.

However, I do recommend blending on a regular basis too because we still need fibre to keep our colon healthy. Fibre helps to pull toxins out of the body, through the colon and into the toilet. Fibre is also imperative to feed those *pro*biotics (good bacteria). Remember fibre is also known as a *pre*biotic.

Chapter 28
Why Greens Are Important for Our Beauty and Health

Green vegetables are the foods most commonly missing in modern diets today. Learning to incorporate dark leafy greens into your daily routine is essential to establishing a healthy, beautiful, strong body and immune system. When you nourish yourself with greens, you may naturally crowd out the foods that make you less than beautiful. Greens help build your internal rainforest and strengthen the blood and respiratory system. Leafy green vegetables are also high-alkaline foods, which may be beneficial to people exposed to higher amounts of pollution in urban areas. The alkaline minerals in our bodies are used to neutralise acidic conditions caused by the environment. Green vegetables will help to replenish our alkaline mineral stores and continue to filter out pollutants.

Green is associated with Spring, the time of renewal, refreshment and vital energy. In Traditional Chinese Medicine, green is related to the liver, emotional stability and creativity.

Nutritionally, greens are very high in calcium, magnesium, iron, potassium, phosphorous, zinc and vitamins A, C, E and K. They are loaded with fibre, folic acid, chlorophyll and many other micronutrients and phytochemicals. Although choosing organic is recommended, eating non-organic greens is still preferable to not eating any greens at all! Some of the proven and possible benefits of consuming dark leafy greens are:

- Blood purification
- Cancer prevention
- Improved circulation

- Strengthened immune system
- Promotion of healthy intestinal flora
- Promotion of subtle, light and flexible energy
- Improved liver, gall bladder and kidney function
- Glowing skin
- Anti-aging
- Cleared congestion, especially in lungs by reducing mucus.

There are a wide variety of greens to choose from, so try to find options that you will enjoy and eat often. Be adventurous and explore new greens that you've never tried before. Try to include Bok Choy; Cabbage; Kale; Collards; Watercress; Mustard Greens; Dandelion and other dark leafy greens. Spinach, Swiss chard and beet greens are best eaten in moderation because they are high in oxalic acid, which inhibits the absorption of the calcium these foods contain. However, rotating between varieties of green vegetables shouldn't cause any nutritional consequences in regards to calcium. It's always good to rotate your greens. Try a new one every week.

Always make sure you get dark leafy greens. The more bitter the better.

AND get LOTS of CELERY! It is one of the best sources of potassium, sodium and sulphur. These are the 3 most needed minerals in the human body. It is one of the most healing and beautifying foods, and very high in electrolytes. **Make celery juice the base of every juice you make. You can have celery every day.**

As you are aware, my favourite way to incorporate greens into the diet is by juicing and blending. Also, at every meal you should be eating greens either as a starter or filling ½ of your plate with a green, raw salad or green vegetables. Lightly steamed vegetables are also a great option. The most important thing – you have to have greens EVERYDAY!

'When you are green inside, you are clean inside.'

Try This Juice Recipe:

- 2 green apples
- 2 kale leaves
- Handful of spinach
- Handful of parsley
- ½ lemon
- Send all ingredients through a juicer.

The more dark-leafy greens we can get into our bodies the better. They are also an excellent source of the mineral zinc; which allows new collagen to form. Bye-bye wrinkles and hello beautiful skin.

Chapter 29
What Does Chlorophyll Do?

> **The MOST IMPORTANT REASON to take in more GREENS is for their CHLOROPHYLL content.**

Chlorophyll is responsible for the green pigmentation in plants BUT it also keeps our bodies beautiful and healthy. It is something that is missing from most of our diets today. We need it!

Chlorophyll is what absorbs energy from the sun to facilitate photosynthesis in plants. Chlorophyll to plants is like blood to humans. Interestingly, chlorophyll is chemically similar in composition to that of human blood, except that the central atom in chlorophyll is magnesium, while iron is central in human blood. Chlorophyll has been seen to provide health benefits to those who take it daily. It has anti-oxidant, anti-inflammatory and wound-healing properties.

> "Chlorophyll is a detoxifier; it's a deodorant and an outstanding healer. Green is clean, it is pure sap of the Earth and it rebuilds our blood; it actually remakes our blood. Our blood is centred on iron, chlorophyll is centred on magnesium; very interesting research in that area as to if there really is a difference between chlorophyll and haemoglobin. Not much of a difference."
> – David Wolfe

Here are a few good reasons why you should be eating, juicing or blending greens EVERYDAY:

1. **Antioxidant Powerhouse** Antioxidants are key fighters of oxidative damage. Over time, free radicals wreak havoc on the body and lead to a number of different degenerative diseases such as cancer. Since we are exposed to millions of free radicals on a daily basis, the only way to combat them is to consume an antioxidant-rich diet. Chlorophyll protects against free radical damage at the cellular level, which in turn can protect the body from developing the degenerative effects of oxidative stress over time. Without antioxidants we will also rapidly age.

2. **Blood Booster** Chlorophyll closely resembles red blood cells. On a molecular level, red blood cells and chlorophyll are virtually identical except for one atom. Chlorophyll helps to replenish our red blood cell count by providing a continuous boost of energy to the bloodstream. When our red blood cell count is high, more oxygen can circulate throughout the body, which is key for the proper health and function of the bodily systems. This also means glowing skin.

3. **Cleansing** Our bodies are bombarded with toxins on a regular basis, which over time can lead to numerous diseases and conditions. Chlorophyll has the ability to bind with many of these toxins and dangerous heavy metals such as lead, mercury, aluminium etc. and remove them from the body. Heavy metal toxicity is also a number one cause in autoimmune diseases today.

4. **Combats Body Odour** Bad breath and body odour are an embarrassing part of human nature, and are often caused by internal issues. Chlorophyll can combat embarrassing odours thanks to antibacterial capabilities that target the internal source of the problem.

5. **Cancer Prevention** Research suggests the antioxidant capabilities of chlorophyll can protect against numerous types of cancer throughout the body.

6. **Counteracts Diet Dilemmas** When you just can't say no to sugar or high fat greasy fried foods, snacking on some chlorophyll-rich leafy greens may just help counteract your poor diet choices. Fried foods contain chemicals that can damage the lining of the colon and

up your risk for developing colon cancer. Colon cancer is also on the rise today. Ditch the fried foods and eat more greens. Leafy greens also help to curb sugar cravings.

7. **A Natural Healer** Chlorophyll has long been touted for its healing properties, both internal and external. Aside from supplying your body with numerous antioxidants to combat internal stresses, when applied topically to wounds, chlorophyll decreases the healing time and reduces the risk of infection, thanks to its antibacterial and antifungal properties.

8. Chlorophyll helps in neutralizing the pollution that we breathe in and intake every day – a good supplement for smokers. It efficiently delivers magnesium and helps the blood in carrying the much needed oxygen to all cells and tissues.

9. Along with other vitamins such as A, C and E, chlorophyll has been seen to help neutralize free radicals that do damage to healthy cells. Anti-aging.

10. It has anti-mutagenic and anti-carcinogenic properties so it may be helpful in protecting your body against toxins and in reducing drug side effects.

While you can get chlorophyll from leafy greens, 3 of the absolute best sources are chlorella, spirulina and marine phytoplankton. These are all algae's from the sea and are some of my favourite superfoods. Greens such as parsley, spinach, kale, and beet tops are also rich in chlorophyll. Wheatgrass is another good choice.

Chapter 30
Blue-Green Algae for Beauty and the GUT

What Is It?

It is a form of bacteria. Blue-green algae is one of the most nutrient dense foods on the planet and is a great prebiotic to feed the beneficial microbes in the gut. My favourites are spirulina and chlorella. Known to be high in iron; vitamin B12; calcium; niacin; potassium; magnesium; beta-carotene and B vitamins. They are also known to destroy cancer cells. It's pretty powerful stuff!

Spirulina as well as chlorella not only enhance probiotics in the gut but they also protect good bacteria in the gut from being killed off. Radiation, heavy metals and toxins can destroy probiotics in the gut; however spirulina and chlorella protect the digestive tract against this. Having heavy metals in the gut (lead, mercury, aluminium etc.) is also a root cause of inflammation and autoimmune disease. We need to try our best to eliminate them.

Both of these algae's help to cleanse and detoxify the body. They are known to pull heavy metals out of the body and heal the intestinal lining (leaky gut).

Spirulina reduces inflammation in the body and is even known to help with weight loss and killing candida. I highly recommend you take one of these daily in a smoothie or with coconut water/apple juice to take away the taste. It may be quite strong if you aren't used to it. Try to alternate daily between the 2, or you can have both in a day, sometimes I do. They are equally beneficial to good health and beauty.

See chlorella as your new multivitamin. Algaes are known to be one of the most complete foods on this planet. You would be able to survive only on this. Pretty good stuff right?

Chlorella is a complete protein, this means it has ALL the amino acids, plus all kinds of minerals, enzymes, chlorophyll, beta-carotene, vitamins C, E, K, B complex, RNA, DNA, folic acid, biotin, choline, phosphorous, magnesium, germanium, sulphur, iron, calcium, manganese, copper, zinc, iodine and cobalt. All of these are BEAUTY MINERALS, which means chlorella is your go to for glowing, gorgeous skin. A wonderful anti-aging superfood.

It also grows healthy bacteria in our gut. Remember, we need a healthy microbiome in order to achieve beautiful skin and amazing health. When the gut is healthy this means our immune system is also strong, which keeps our body running in tip top condition.

Since chlorella is a detoxifying food, you can eat as much as you want without any fear of it becoming toxic. It is also known to help fight cellulite.

Algaes are also a rich source of omega-3 fatty acids, which is needed to keep our hormones healthy.

My favourite green smoothie recipe to take daily for glowing skin and good health is:

Ingredients:

- 1 ½ cups of water or fresh (Thai) coconut water.
- 2 big handfuls of spinach, kale, romaine lettuce or any other greens.
- 4 stalks of celery.
- 1 organic apple, or chopped kiwi or green pear.
- Juice of ½ fresh lemon or lime.
- 2 baby cucumbers with skin left on (only buy organic cucumbers).
- 1 handful of fresh herbs e.g. parsley, mint etc. (you decide).
- 1 inch of fresh ginger root.
- Optional add a green protein powder of your choice; for example, spirulina or wheatgrass.

- Blend all together and serve.

> **Drink GREEN every day. This is one of the best ways to stay younger and healthy.**

Rotate greens each week so you are getting a different variety. They all have different minerals and vitamins that your body needs. No green has the same nutritional content.

Chapter 31
The Amazing Powers of Turmeric for Beauty and the GUT

In Ayurvedic medicine, turmeric is considered a 'cleanser of the body'. It has very potent medicinal properties, known as 'curcumoids' with powerful anti-inflammatory effects; it is also recognised as a strong antioxidant. It is so powerful that it matches the effectiveness of some anti-inflammatory drugs.

Turmeric is known to destroy all inflammation in the body. When you are inflamed, your detoxification pathways are suppressed. And when this happens, toxins begin to build up in your body leading to even more problems. We now know that all inflammation begins in the GUT!

Turmeric is known to make the skin soft, supple and smooth. To get beautiful skin you must have clean blood. Turmeric helps to purify the blood, helping with acne and other skin conditions. It is known to make your skin more radiant. Curcumin has become very popular today as an anti-aging supplement.

Research also shows that turmeric is a powerful weapon against depression and anxiety as it helps to balance serotonin. Serotonin your 'happy hormone' is 90% produced in the gut. It is responsible for maintaining mood balance; this is what makes us feel happy. If serotonin levels fall off, we may experience anxiety and depression. Depression is a brain disorder but it comes from the gut (inflammation travels to the brain via the vagus nerve). Turmeric not only boosts serotonin levels but it also heals the gut and switches off any inflammation. Remember, the root cause of almost everything is inflammation. When serotonin levels are high, skin is known to be healthy and glows naturally from within. Dark chocolate is also known to boost serotonin levels. Yay to chocolate! Curcumin can also heal damage caused by heavy metal toxicity. Our bodies are polluted today with heavy metals such has mercury, fluoride, chlorine etc.; we have to take in more foods that are going to help eliminate them from our body. Heavy metals are also another cause of autoimmune diseases. Curcumin may also help heal a leaky gut.

Here Are Some More AMAZING Benefits Of Turmeric:

- It helps to detoxify the blood by producing enzymes that break down toxins in the body.
- It may help prevent and improve Alzheimer's disease. This is also known to be caused by inflammation in the gut (vagus nerve).
- Helps with digestive disorders, soothes stomach, relaxes muscles, and helps with cramps.
- Can combat heart disease.
- Helps to alleviate rheumatoid arthritis – a chronic inflammation disorder that affects and destroys the joints, cartilage and bone (and helps with autoimmune diseases).

How To Use Turmeric:

- Sprinkle on to your food.
- Juice it or blend it. (If you can find the root, juice it or even grate into tea, watch out for orange fingers).
- Drink it as a tea.
- Take as a supplement.
- Have as a shot with black pepper and coconut oil. (Ideally, turmeric should be taken with black pepper and an oil such as coconut as it is fat soluble, this means it needs a healthy fat alongside it to be absorbed fully in the body). 1 tsp. turmeric, ½ tsp. black pepper and 1tsp to 1 tbsp. of coconut oil in warm water first thing in the morning or before bed.

What Can You Expect If You Take Turmeric Daily?

- Less pain and stiffness in your joints.
- Better sleep quality.
- Improved mental clarity.
- More balanced mood.
- Smoother digestion.
- Clearer, more radiant, glowing skin.
- It is also known as a help in curing and preventing cancer. That's right! This stuff is powerful.

Chapter 32
Sprouts and Their Amazing Beauty and Health Benefits

I have dedicated a whole chapter to 'sprouts' because I believe they are so beneficial to our health and beauty needs.
Now I don't mean Brussels sprouts, although these are good too, I'm talking about sprouted seeds such as mung beans, adzuki, beetroot, alfalfa, broccoli etc.

Sprouts are germinated seeds of legumes or grains. In naturopathy, sprouts are referred to as a 'medicine'. Many health practitioners believe that sprouts are one of the greatest healing foods.

They have a significant amount of vitamins and nutrients than they do in an un-sprouted form. A week after sprouting, the sprouts will have the highest concentration and bioavailability of nutrients. Beans must contain a packed storehouse of all the important nutrients that a plant will need to grow in its initial days, so those tiny caps are filled with important organic compounds, vitamins, and minerals that our body can also utilize.

The health and beauty benefits of sprouts are pretty amazing.

They include the ability to:

- Improve the digestive process
- Boost the metabolism / helping with weight loss
- Purify blood – clean blood means glowing skin
- Increase enzymatic activity throughout the body
- Prevent anaemia

- Lower cholesterol
- Reduce blood pressure
- Protect against cancer
- Boost skin health – great for acne sufferers and more
- Boost the condition of your hair
- Improve vision
- Support the immune system and
- Help to give you more energy.

The important thing to remember is that much of the nutritive value of sprouts is lost when they are heated. They should always be added to meals in their raw form to guarantee that they have the most impact.

Sprouts contain a high amount of protein and fibre, as well as vitamin K, folate, pantothenic acid, niacin, thiamine (vitamin B1), vitamin C, vitamin A, and riboflavin. In terms of minerals, sprouts contain manganese, copper, zinc, magnesium, iron, and calcium.

Many of these nutrients increase dramatically as the sprout continues to develop. Along with all of those components, sprouts are also a rich source of enzymes that are essential for health and beauty. Enzymes are what keep us young and beautiful!

Sprouts and Their Benefits:

1. Good Digestion

Sprouts contain a high number of enzymes. This can help boost the various metabolic processes and chemical reactions within the body, specifically when it comes to digestion. We now know that enzymes are an important part of the digestive process, helping to break down food effectively, increasing the absorption of nutrients by the digestive tract. The dietary fibre also found in sprouts makes it a very important boost for digestive functions. Remember, fibre is needed to feed your probiotics. Fibre also bulks up the stool, making it easier to pass through the digestive tract, which can help with constipation, as well as diarrhoea, and may even prevent bowel/colon cancer.

2. Boost Metabolism – helpful for weight loss

As was already mentioned, sprouts contain an abundance of enzymes. These can seriously impact the metabolic activity of your body (in a good way). Sprouts also contain protein, (amino acids). Amino acids are necessary for almost all bodily processes, particularly the creation and maintenance of cells, organ repair, skin regeneration, bone growth, muscle development, and a number of other very important aspects of health and beauty.

3. Anaemia and Blood Circulation

Anaemia is another word for an iron deficiency. If you do not consume enough food with iron, your red blood cell count drops, because iron is an essential part of red blood cell production. This can result in fatigue, lack of concentration, nausea, light-headedness, and stomach disorders. By maintaining your red blood cell count with proper amounts of iron (and copper, which is also found in sprouts), you can improve the circulation of blood in your body, thereby increasing the oxygenation of organ systems and cells to optimize their performance. An important point to note, if you have a leaky gut you may not be absorbing iron from the foods you eat. You MUST heal and seal your gut.

4. Weight Loss

As previously mentioned sprouts help to boost metabolism due to their high enzyme content but they also help you to lose weight as they are very high in nutrients but low in calories. This means that you can eat as many sprouts as you wish without worrying about your weight. The fibre in sprouts also helps to keep you feeling full. This can reduce overeating and snacking.

5. Heart Health

Sprouts are a great source of omega-3 fatty acids. Omega-3 fatty acids are anti-inflammatory, which keeps our body and skin in tip-top health. Sprouts are also high in potassium, which helps to reduce blood pressure. This keeps our heart healthy.

6. Immune System

Sprouts are full of vitamin C making them a powerful stimulant for the white blood cells in the body to fight off infection and disease. Vitamin C is also needed to help synthesise collagen. Collagen keeps our skin youthful. As a sprout continues to develop, vitamin A also multiplies. Vitamin A is needed for your body to grow and repair itself. It also supports a healthy immune system, helps you maintain good eyesight and helps your intestines absorb zinc. Vitamin A is also needed for beautiful skin.

7. Cancer Prevention

Free radicals are the natural, dangerous by-products of cellular metabolism that can cause healthy cells to mutate into cancerous cells. They are also responsible for some heart diseases, premature aging, cognitive decline, and a variety of age-related health concerns. Sprouts can counteract these effects, thereby helping to reduce the chances of developing cancer.

8. Cold Sores

Cold sores can be an unsightly, painful, and an uncomfortable condition to suffer through. If they get infected, they can even become a serious health risk. There is a specific enzyme, called lysine that actually inhibits the growth of cold sores and treats them if they do appear. Guess what! This enzyme is found in significant amounts in sprouts.

9. Allergy and Asthma

Some varieties of sprouts, like broccoli sprouts, have been linked to reducing allergic reactions, including asthma, which is an inflammatory condition of the respiratory system. Another interesting fact is that a lack of good bacteria in the gut is also linked to allergies and asthma.

Sprouts for Beautiful Hair

As mentioned sprouts contain a decent amount of vitamin C and protein, which is proven to promote healthy hair growth. Vitamin C destroys free radicals in the body, which makes the hair weak, brittle and thin. It also prevents a variety of hair disorders like alopecia. Sprouts also improve blood circulation and strengthens and repairs capillaries, which helps us to get strong and thick hair. A healthy blood supply is a good stimulant for hair growth.

The high amounts of vitamin A in sprouts stimulate hair follicles and encourage the scalp to produce more hair. Vitamin A deficiency can lead to dry scalp, roots and strands, leading to hair loss. Proper levels of vitamin A are essential to encourage healthy hair growth. A key note to remember is, if you have any gut disorder you also need vitamin A to support healing.

One cause of premature greying hair is due to the oxidation of tissues. The potent antioxidants present in the sprouts prevent the corrosion of tissues, reducing the possibility of premature hair greying. By consuming sprouts regularly, you may be able to reverse grey hair.

Sprouts also contain vitamin K (a beauty enhancer), fat soluble vitamin, which builds protein in the scalp to maintain strong roots and strands. They contain huge amounts of iron, which are required to carry oxygen to the scalp, roots and tresses. Hair that is starved from proper levels of iron may weaken and fall out. Sprouts also contain zinc, a nutrient which, contributes to sebum production in the scalp. This keeps the scalp, roots and hair strands hydrated. It also promotes regeneration of the scalp cells. Once again zinc is essential for a healthy gut.

Selenium in sprouts helps to kill off dandruff, removing the debris to encourage new hair growth. Selenium is also needed for a healthy gut and thyroid. If your thyroid isn't working, well you may notice your hair becoming thinner, dry or brittle. This is one sign you may have a thyroid problem.

Regular consumption of sprouts may also add shine, elasticity and lustre to the hair as they contain omega-3 fatty acids as mentioned previously.

Sprouts are known to also help correct/balance hormonal issues, which is one of the biggest causes of hair loss in women and men. A great food for PCOS sufferers too.

Sprouts contain Biotin. A deficiency in this vitamin can cause brittle damaged hair; therefore, you need to eat sprouts for gorgeous, long, lustrous locks.

As you can see sprouts contain almost every mineral and vitamin our body's need for gorgeous hair. You can even juice them.

Skin Benefits of Sprouts

1. Glowing Skin

Sprouts are an amazing beauty food that can help your skin glow from the inside out.

Pea sprouts are known to be rich in vitamin B, which prevents excess sebum production and helps in healthy skin formation. Drink a glass of pea sprout juice daily to get a well-hydrated and moisturised skin.

2. Cell Regeneration

Include sprouts in your daily diet to increase the process of healing and rejuvenation of the skin. They also help to heal the wound at a faster pace and replace damaged tissue. They lighten skin discoloration like freckles and age spots to get a clear and flawless skin.

3. Stimulate Collagen Production

The vitamin C in sprouts promotes better skin through the production of collagen. It provides elasticity to give you more youthful skin, rejuvenating the skin from within, and reducing wrinkles and other signs of aging.

4. Acne Buster

As we know now sprouts contain high levels of omega-3 fatty acids. This decreases inflammation in the body and when the body is less inflamed this reduces the risk of acne and other skin problems. Consuming enough sprouts daily will help give you a smoother, younger looking skin with a reduction in inflammatory conditions like acne, eczema, psoriasis etc. Omega-3 is important in the quest for beautiful skin and to delay aging.

5. Detoxifies the System

Sprouts contain silica a mineral which is required to rebuild and regenerate the skin's connective tissues. Silica is also known as another 'beauty mineral'. It is also helpful at removing toxins from the body that could seep into the bloodstream causing dull, wrinkled and lifeless skin.

6. Prevent Premature Aging

Sprouts contain an abundance of highly active antioxidants that prevent DNA destruction and protect us from the ongoing effects of aging. At the end of your DNA we have telomeres. If these erode, we age. Your job is to prevent these telomeres from eroding by eating powerful anti-inflammatory foods that preserve our youth. Sprouts are one of them.

7. Pregnancy

Though sprouts are good for a pregnancy diet, pregnant women need to be careful while consuming sprouts due to bacterial growth. If they are not cleaned and sprouted properly, sprouts pose a risk of salmonella and e-coli, which can cause diarrhoea, nausea, abdominal cramping, fever and other serious illnesses in pregnant women. Pregnant women should opt for cooked sprouts only. Sprouts contain a high amount of folate so they are very beneficial to pregnant women.

Types Of Sprouts:

Adzuki	Chickpea	Lentil
Mustard	Millet	Fenugreek – known for their curative properties.
Sesame	Sunflower	Alfalfa (although they are known to contain mold).
Mung	Green Pea	Broccoli – one of the BEST sprouts. So powerful they can help cure cancer. Great for the skin.
Watercress	Brussels Sprouts – the best sprouts for improving health of hair.	Gram – known for enhancing vigour and vitality.

These are just a few examples of sprouts. There are a lot of different varieties. You can try sprouting your own seeds at home if you have the motivation. Alternatively, you can buy from the supermarket or health food stores and they are sold at a pretty low price.

Chapter 33
Food Combining for a Healthy Gut

Many of us aren't aware but there are certain foods that should not be mixed together. Poorly combined food choices may cause bad digestion; flatulence; bloating; no energy; bad skin and even stop you from losing weight. As we now know digestion takes up a lot of energy so we want to start freeing it up a lot more so we can become more energised and look amazing.

A HEATHY GUT = A HAPPY YOU!

Here Are The Happy Gut Rules:

Carbohydrates and Vegetables YES *(a good mix).*	Example: Brown rice Millet Sweet potatoes Parsnips Squash Potatoes Pasta etc. These all mix well with vegetables. (E.g. pasta and broccoli together are a good mix.)
Fats and Carbohydrates YES *(a good mix).*	As mentioned above for carbs. Healthy fats such as avocado, nuts etc. (E.g. avocado with brown rice cakes).

Protein and Protein NO (They do not mix well).	Rule of thumb eat only one protein at a meal. Protein is really hard for your body to break down and may cause digestive issues if you consume a lot together in one sitting.
Proteins and Carbohydrates NO *The digestion of these 2 food groups are different. If you eat them together, they may cause digestion issues.*	Animal proteins are very hard to break down in our body. They require a lot of energy and digestion so best to not eat with other food, unless it's a green salad or vegetables. Protein should be eaten with fibre (greens).
Protein and Vegetables YES *(a good mix).*	Vegetables are fairly easy to digest; therefore your body can focus more on digesting the animal protein. (E.g. chicken and broccoli).
Fruits should always be eaten on an empty stomach.	Always make it a rule to have fruit alone or before a meal. It ferments in your stomach and causes bad digestion problems if you eat after a meal. Food that ferments inside you creates gas.

Chapter 34
Facial Mapping

Look at your face if you want to see how healthy and beautiful you are on the inside.

Each line, spot on your face etc. all link to a certain organ in your body.

The Chinese believe that you can tell a lot about the health of your body simply by looking at your face.

> **Your face is an indication of your true beauty and health within.**

A lined forehead or breakouts (Bladder and/or Small Intestine).	This could mean a blocked or toxic colon and gallbladder. May be caused by eating too much dairy, processed meat, takeaways, cooked oils or processed food. A sign that your body is toxic.
Dark circles under the eyes or puffiness.	Can be your kidneys and adrenals are exhausted. Maybe caused by too much caffeine, a lack of sleep, not enough water, medication or too much stress.
Crow's feet around the eyes.	Can also be adrenal exhaustion or your body is too acidic. Clean your

	liver to deal with crow's feet. The Chinese believe that fine lines and wrinkles are a vitamin and mineral deficiency.
Deep laugh lines around the mouth.	Linked to the lungs and liver. Maybe due to smoking or shallow chest breathing. Not enough oxygen is getting into the lungs. (Take up yoga for this). Possibly also linked to the colon. It is backed up with fermenting food or the liver isn't working very well. The deeper the grooves, the more messed up the colon.
Breakouts around the chin/jaw (Hormones).	Eating too much fat or sweet food. Eating hormone injected meat and dairy. Lack of water. Possibly a congested colon or kidney issues. Can also be linked to stress and unbalanced hormones.
Lines above the upper lip (Stomach).	Around the mouth area relates to the stomach and intestines. Possibly a blocked digestive tract (unless you are a smoker. Smoking causes these too).
Lines or breakouts around the cheekbones (Lungs and Kidneys).	Smoking, eating too much animal protein / animal products etc. Stress.
Frown lines between eyebrows.	Liver issues or you could just be frowning a lot.

This is just a small look into facial mapping. Have a look online if you would like to learn more about it.

Chapter 35
Essential Oils for Outstanding Beauty and Health

Most of today's commercial beauty products are full of chemicals and toxins such as parabens and phthalates that seep into your blood causing inflammation. They also contain heavy metals such as mercury, lead, and aluminium. This may then lead to chronic diseases such as autoimmunes and even cancer, as well as premature aging and bad skin. If you slather these products onto your skin every single day, eventually, your kidneys will also be in trouble. As the kidneys become overloaded with these poisonous chemicals, dark circles may appear under the eyes and you may find yourself fatigued all day long with early signs of aging beginning to appear too. We need to look to more natural alternatives to heal the body and skin from the outside in.

Cleopatra was considered to be the most beautiful woman in the world. She was known to use essential oils on her skin such as rose, frankincense, cypress, neroli and myrhh. These oils are known to make you more beautiful. I wish I had have known more about essential oils when I was suffering with acne as I could have prevented the scarring I currently have today. Certain oils also help to balance any hormonal issues, which is also needed for acne sufferers.

When looking for oils make sure they are certified organic, cold pressed. These have the greatest healing powers.

Essential Oils Are Known To Help:

- Fight cold and flu symptoms
- Relax your body and soothe sore muscles

- Heal skin conditions such as acne, eczema etc.
- Alleviate pain
- Balance hormones
- Improve digestion
- Reduce cellulite and wrinkles
- Clean your home
- Calm anxiety and stress
- Rejuvenate and heal the body from the outside in
- And MORE!

> **Aromatherapy is one of the most popular forms of natural healthcare. They treat the whole person – body, mind and spirit.**

An essential oil is the natural fragrant, essence extracted from flowers, leaves, bark, roots, fruit peel and berries. They are SO powerful to the human body.

Here is a selection of a few of my favourite essential oils that will help to heal, calm the skin and make you more beautiful, healthy and glowing from the outside in.

1. Roman Chamomile
This is particularly effective at treating irritated, itchy skin or rashes. Chamomile can relieve eczema, dryness and stressed skin. Women's health tip; it eases menstrual cramps and also helps with emotional upsets.

2. Frankincense
One of the most important oils for improving skin tone and treating aging skin and wrinkles. Can also reduce scar tissue, helping to close and heal wounds. This is a wonderful, rejuvenating and uplifting oil. Reduces inflammation and age spots and has powerful anti-cancer properties. Known to treat stress, anxiety and tension when inhaled. If taken internally may also heal a leaky gut but you must use a carrier oil such as fractionated coconut oil.

3. Geranium

I love this smell. It is very uplifting and strengthening, great to take you out of a bad mood. Geranium can help to regulate sebum production, which is helpful for both oily and dry skin conditions. It is antiseptic and anti-inflammatory, helping to control acne but equally cooling and moisturising for dry, inflamed skin. This oil may decrease the appearance of wrinkles and can also be used to reduce inflammation. A great oil for people who are prone to anxiety or panic attacks. Give it a sniff when you feel a panic attack coming on. Known to also boost the lymphatic system and encourage elimination of toxins. Good for cellulite.

4. Grapefruit

Cooling has gently antiseptic properties that treat oily skin, opening pores and acne. Can help to tone and tighten loose skin. Supports metabolism and cellulite reduction when mixed with coconut oil and applied to areas of cellulite. If rubbed into the gut, it also helps also to relieve constipation.

5. Lemongrass

Cleans the lymphatic system and functions as a natural deodoriser. Can relieve stress and nervous exhaustion. Tones a sluggish digestive system.

6. Immortelle

Anti-inflammatory has regenerative properties, making it useful for scars, acne, dermatitis, stretch marks, bruises, boils and abscesses. Also a wonderful anti-aging oil.

7. Juniper Berry

Famed for helping to heal eczema and psoriasis. As a skin toner it aids the treatment of clogged, oily and unhealthy skin or skin prone to blackheads and acne. A helpful diuretic, to encourage elimination of toxins; another good one for cellulite.

8. Lemon

Has a clarifying effect as well as toning properties that help combat wrinkles and spider veins. May help to tighten the appearance of the skin. Improves lymph drainage cleanses the body, reducing cellulite and fluid retention. Supports a healthy liver function.

9. Mandarin

With its astringent properties, it makes a good toner for oily skin. Helps tone loose skin. Helps to also relieve constipation if rubbed over the stomach. Helps to calm the nerves and comforts the emotions.

10. Myrrh

Can delay the forming of wrinkles and other signs of aging skin. A natural antiseptic, can prevent or reduce infections. Helps to keep the skin looking healthy. Reduces stretch marks, and improves hormonal balance. Rubbed over abdomen treats sluggish digestion and wind. Good for diarrhoea.

11. Palmarosa

Has a balancing and hydrating effect on all skin types, helpful for acne and other minor skin infections. Stimulates cellular regeneration and can reduce wrinkles, scar tissue, stretch marks and improve the appearance of tired or aging skin. Aids digestion and helps to rebalance intestinal flora after infection or antibiotics. Helpful for stress and anxiety.

12. Sandalwood

This oil is effective for nourishing dry skin. It also protects the skin against impurities from pollution and unwanted microbes, making it also handy for acne-prone skin.

13. Rose

Most commonly treated for dry, mature skin. However, Rose is useful for all ages and offers strong antibacterial action to help fight acne. When massaged into the skin can reduce scarring. It also helps to reduce stress, PMT or painful periods.

14. Lavender

Extremely useful for wounds, ulcers and sores of all kinds. It helps to clear up acne, psoriasis and scarring. One of the only few oils that can be applied directly to the skin. Good for digestive problems and of course it is known as the oil that helps you sleep.

The Best Carrier Oils

Most oils (with the exception of lavender) should NEVER be applied directly onto your skin, Always use a carrier oil before application. Here are a few of my favourites:

1. **Sweet Almond** – high in essential fatty acids and antioxidants to nourish the skin. Known to help with puffy eyes.
2. **Argan** – ideal for healing, soothing and moisturising the skin. High in omega fatty acids and vitamin E. Also a good oil to nourish the hair, apply to hair tips.
3. **Jojoba** – nourishing. Good for treating acne and oily skin as well as dry and dehydrated skin.
4. **Coconut** – containing potent fatty acids to replenish your skin. Coconut oil is naturally antibacterial so great when dealing with acne but is also anti-aging.
5. **Avocado** – contains vitamin E to boost overall skin health and promote anti-aging.
6. **Evening Primrose** – high in vitamin E and beneficial for psoriasis and eczema. A good oil to calm any inflammation of the skin.
7. **Rosehip Seed** – a rich oil that encourages growth and repair of skin tissue. Particularly helpful for reducing scar tissue and healing sun damaged skin, as well as smoothing fine lines, wrinkles and general skin aging. This oil always makes my skin look plumper when I wake up the next day.
8. **Macadamia** – is moisturising, makes your skin really soft. It is anti-aging, slowing down the rate of maturity of the skin, keeping it youthful and supple. I also like to apply this oil to the tips of my hair.
9. **Grapeseed** – helps with skin conditions such as acne and spots. Helps to prevent the pores from clogging. Regular application of this oil can help tighten the skin. Also look out for new oils on the shelves such as baobab, melon seed and cacay. These are also great. There are many to choose from and they are so much better for your health and your skin than commercial bought beauty products.

How To Use Essential Oils:

A good starting point is 1-2 drops of essential oil per tablespoon of carrier oil.

Rub into your skin and leave on overnight to rejuvenate and make yourself more beautiful and glowing.

I like to add 1-2 drops to my body moisturiser or coconut oil also to make me smell nice and to get those extra health and beauty benefits in.

You can also add a couple of drops into your favourite shampoo to help nourish the hair and scalp.

Essential oils and carrier oils can make a big change to your skin in a positive way. Throw out your toxic beauty care products and invest in these. You'll be glad you did.

Chapter 36
Yoga and Breath for a Healthy Gut

Do you ever notice how you are breathing? I bet not many of you do. Well I want you to start paying attention to your breath.

Breathing is a basic human function, but not everyone breathes effectively, especially during stressful times. By practicing proper breathing techniques, you can reduce stress and improve your body's overall functioning.

Learning how to breathe correctly can change your health and beauty in so many ways. Here are a few reasons why:

1. **Your respiratory system works better**. Respiratory difficulties such as asthma, bronchitis and even chest pain can subside with correct breathing.

2. **Your digestive system works properly.** Constipation is very common and is often due to shallow breathing. When people learn to breathe into their lower abdomen they begin to have regular bowel movements straight away. Breathing into the gut massages the internal organs to function well. It calms the emotions, which directly affects the digestion system.

3. **Your lymph system works well**. Correct breathing increases circulation of lymphatic fluid (again think cellulite).

4. **Your circulation system moves well**. Oxygen can flow freely to the heart. Blood can circulate, relieving congestion throughout the body. This also means glowing skin.

5. **Your immune system has more energy**. Helps tissues to regenerate and heal.

6. **Your nervous system is calmer**. Anxiety can be reversed by deep-breathing. Great for stress.
7. **It can lengthen your telomeres** and provide a dramatic boost in serotonin. Telomeres are what keep us looking younger for longer.

Every cell in your body needs a supply of oxygen. High concentrations of oxygen are also anti-inflammatory and trigger the body's natural healing functions. It is imperative you are taking in enough oxygen daily.

Breathing Technique

Remember, oxygen is one of the MOST important nutrients for your body. It helps your body absorb vitamins, minerals and nutrients more efficiently and it can speed up the cleaning process. Oxygen also stimulates collagen and elastin production plus hair thrives with a rich supply of oxygenated blood. We must learn how to breathe correctly. Here is how:

Learn to breathe from the belly (the diaphragm). To tell whether or not you are breathing into your diaphragm, place one hand onto your upper chest, and the other hand onto your belly, just below your rib cage. Breathe in slowly through your nose (nasal breathing brings more oxygen into the body, breathing from the mouth can dry up the lungs), until you feel your belly start to rise. Try to make sure that your chest remains still, and that it is not moving upward. When your belly is as full of air as possible, (imagine you are filling a balloon up with air), start to tighten your stomach muscles. This will force air slowly from your diaphragm and out of your lungs. Then, exhale through your mouth or your nose. Empty out every last breath from your stomach. This is how you should be breathing daily.

If you are like me and can't fall asleep at night easily, try this breathing technique before bed. Breathe in through the nose for 4 seconds, hold the breath for seven seconds, exhale for 8 seconds, and repeat 3 more times. This exercise will slow down the heart rate and prepare the body for relaxation.

Yoga is a great way to connect to your breath and I highly recommend you start taking classes on a regular basis or even just a couple of times per week to get started.

Here are few yoga poses to help keep your digestion and gut healthy. Most of these will also help your skin to glow too and may even decrease that pesky cellulite.

Wide Legged Child's Pose – creates heat in the stomach area, letting your digestive juices flow. A great pose when you are feeling very stressed out, super calming for the mind.

1. Spread your knees wide apart while keeping your big toes touching.
2. Rest your buttocks on your heels.
3. Forward fold over your thighs and knees so your forehead touches the floor.
4. Close your eyes and begin to breathe in and out through the nose for around 10 breaths. Make sure your breath is coming from the belly, not the chest.

Cat/Cow – massages digestive organs, increasing blood flow to intestinal area. This asana flow is known to tone the gastrointestinal tract and female reproductive system as well as helping to relieve stress from menstrual cramps, lower back pain, and sciatica.

1. Position yourself on the mat on your hands and knees, wrists directly under your shoulders, knees hip-width apart and directly under your hips.
2. Inhale deeply and then exhale as you lift and curve your back upward, dropping your head down and curling your tailbone under.
3. Now inhale as you reverse the spinal curve, lifting your tailbone, drawing your shoulders back, and raising your chest and head as far as you can as your spine softens and your abdominal muscles relax.
4. Continue the flow for at least 5-10 breaths.

Extended Puppy Pose – stretches the stomach muscles. This is excellent for cramps that are associated with constipation and poor digestion. Relieves symptoms of chronic stress, tension and insomnia.

1. Come to all fours (table top position) with your shoulders stacked over your wrists, your hips stacked over your knees, and the tops of your feet relaxed down on the mat.
2. Slowly begin to walk your hands out in front of you, lowering your chest down toward the ground.
3. Keep your hips over your knees and your arms shoulder distance apart, and gently release your forehead down to the ground.
4. Activate your arms by pressing into the palms of your hands and lifting your elbows and forearms away from the ground.
5. Draw your shoulder blades onto your back and reach your hips up high toward the ceiling.
6. Hold for 30 seconds – 1 minute.

Downward Facing Dog – relaxes the gastrointestinal tract. It also boosts circulation making it a wonderful anti-aging pose. A fantastic pose to calm down the mind as it helps you to focus on your breathing. I like to inhale through the nose and take a big breath out through the mouth to really de-stress and fully relax the body.

1. Exhale as you press down with your palms and lift from the hips, rolling onto the balls of your feet, and pushing back and up.
2. Feet are hip-width apart, your heels stretch towards the floor and your hips reach toward the sky. Do not worry if your knees are bent. It is better to have bent knees than a rounded back.
3. Hands are shoulder-width apart and your head is gazing to the centre of your feet or navel.
4. Relax into the pose and take 10 cleansing breaths.

Big Toe Pose – contracts the abdominal organs and when released fresh blood rushes to the area. Improves circulation to digestive organs; therefore improving digestion. This pose may help when you are feeling bloated or if you have any trapped gas inside you. A great pose to give you glowing skin too.

1. Slide the index and middle fingers of each hand between the big toes and the second toes.
2. Then curl those fingers under and grip the big toes firmly, wrapping the thumbs around the other 2 fingers to secure the wrap.
3. Press your toes down against your fingers.
4. With an inhalation, lift your torso as if you were going to stand up again, straightening your elbows.
5. Lengthen your front torso, and on the next exhale, lift your sitting bones.
6. Take 10 breaths.

Twisted Lunge – hands to heart. When you are in a twist, you will be essentially compressing your digestive organs. This will cause a lack of circulation. When you release your twist there will be a rush of fresh blood that will flood your digestive organs. Fresh blood flow equals fresh oxygen and nutrients. Twisting will increase blood flow to the digestive organs, thus increasing their ability to function.

1. Come on to the ball of your back foot, lifting your heel and drawing it forward so it aligns directly over your back toes.
2. Lift your back knee and draw your quadriceps up toward the ceiling. Straighten your back leg completely.
3. Keep the ball of your back foot firmly on the ground. With your back leg strong and active, gently draw your left hip forward as you press your right hip back, squaring your hips so they are parallel to the top edge of your mat. If it is too difficult to keep your back leg raised, lower your knee to the floor and slide your leg back a few inches. Un-tuck your back toes and rest the top of your back foot on the floor.
4. Inhale as you raise your torso to an upright position. Sweep your arms overhead. Draw your tailbone toward the floor.

5. Lower your arms and bring your palms together in prayer position at your chest. Exhaling, twist your torso to the right.
6. Bring your left elbow to the outside of your right thigh. Press your upper left arm against your thigh and draw your right shoulder blade into your back to turn your chest to the right.
7. Turn your gaze to the sky. Make sure your front shin stays vertical.
8. Keep your extended leg straight, strong, and lifting. Lengthen your spine even further on your inhalations and twist even deeper on your exhalations.
9. Draw your thumbs to your heart, and heart toward your thumbs.

Twisted Lunge – hands to floor. As mentioned above, when you twist you will cut off blood supply to your digestive organs, and then re-introduce fresh blood to your abdominal organs when you release your twist. This re-introduction of fresh blood can help to cleanse the cells of any built up waste because with increased circulation comes increased cellular detoxification. You can also help to move stagnated impurities and gas through your digestive tract due to the compression that comes with twisting.

1. Same as above but this time release palm to the inner edge of your foot and glide your opposite arm up to the ceiling. Look up.
2. Make sure both shoulders are in line.
3. Take 10 long inhales and exhales.

Twisted Triangle – stimulates the release of toxic waste trapped in the intestines, helping with constipation and digestive problems.

1. Begin standing at the top of your mat with your feet hip-distance apart and your arms at your sides.
2. Step your feet about 2–3 feet apart, and align your heels.
3. Turn your right foot out 90 degrees so your toes are pointing to the top of the mat. The centre of your right kneecap should be aligned with the centre of your right ankle. Pivot your left foot inward to a 45-degree angle.
4. Bring your hands to your hips and square your hips forward.
5. Raise your left arm toward the ceiling, with your bicep next to your left ear. Reach up strongly through your left hand. Inhale.
6. On an exhalation, hinge forward from your hips, keeping your spine long. Place your left hand to the

outside of your right foot as you open your torso to the right.

7. Use your right hand to draw your right hip back so it stays in line with your left hip.

8. Inhale and lengthen your spine again. Then, exhale as you roll your right shoulder back and extend your right arm straight up toward the ceiling. Reach strongly through your right fingertips.

9. Turn your head to gaze at your right thumb.

10. Keep your hips level. Press down firmly through your back heel.

11. Hold the pose for up to one minute. To come out of the pose, gently release the twist. Then, press firmly through your left heel. With an inhalation, lift your torso upright and lower your arms. Turn to the left, reversing the position of your feet, and repeat for the same length of time on the opposite side.

Wind Relief – as it says, relieves trapped wind, known as the gas releasing pose. Massages intestines and abdominal organs. Also great for menstrual cramps. Hold pose for around 10 breaths and then switch legs.

1. Begin by lying on your back, with your legs and arms extended.

2. Take an inhale through your nose and then on your exhale, draw both of your knees to your chest. Clasp your hands around them.

3. While holding only your right shin release your left leg and extend it along the floor (root your left heel into the mat, flexing the toes towards the face). Hold this pose for 10 breaths or up to one minute.

4. Draw your left knee back in towards your chest and clasp your hands around both shins again.

5. While holding only your left shin, release your right leg and extend it along the floor. Hold again for the same amount of time.

6. Finally, draw both knees to your chest.

Knees to chest – great for anyone suffering from IBS; same benefits as wind relieving pose. Also gives lower back a nice massage. Hold for 10 breaths.

Boat – aids healthy digestion. Also helps to deliver fresh blood to the heart, making it both energising and rejuvenating. Great for kidney health too.

1. Begin in a seated position with your knees bent and your feet flat on the floor.

2. Lift your feet off the floor. Keep your knees bent at first. Bring your shins parallel to the floor. This is half boat pose.

3. Your torso will naturally fall back, but do not let the spine round.

4. Straighten your legs to a 45-degree angle if you can do so without losing the integrity of your upper body. You want to keep your torso as upright as possible so that it makes a V shape with the legs.

5. Roll your shoulders back and straighten your arms roughly parallel to the floor with your palms turned up.

6. Balance on the sitting bones.

7. Take 10 breaths.

Half Locust – arms to the side. This pose puts pressure on your digestive organs, helping with gas, constipation and indigestion.

1. Begin lying on your belly with your legs extended straight back behind you, the tops of your feet down, and your chin on your mat.
2. Find a slight internal rotation of your thighs by turning your big toes in toward one another, and keep pressing the tops of your feet down as you lift your kneecaps away from the ground.
3. On an inhale begin to lift up your left leg and point your toes, relax your right leg.
4. Reach the inner lines of your legs toward the ceiling.
5. Keep your chin on the floor, gaze looking forward.
6. Hold for 10 breaths and then switch legs.

Bridge – stimulates and stretches the abdominals, strengthening the core. Also stimulates the thyroid gland, which is needed for digestion, energy, skin health and metabolism.

1. Lie on your back with your knees bent and feet on the floor. Extend your arms along the floor, palms flat.
2. Press your feet and arms firmly into the floor. Take an inhale through the nose and then on the exhale lift your hips toward the ceiling.
3. Draw your tailbone toward your pubic bone, holding your buttocks off the floor. Do not squeeze your glutes or flex your buttocks.
4. Roll your shoulders back and underneath your body. Clasp your hands and extend your arms along the floor beneath your pelvis. Straighten your arms as much as possible, pressing your forearms into the mat. Reach your knuckles toward your heels.
5. Keep your thighs and feet parallel – do not roll to the outer edges of your feet or let your knees drop together. Press your weight evenly across all corners of both feet. Lengthen your tailbone toward the backs of your knees.
6. Hold for up to one minute. To release, unclasp your hands and place your palms-down alongside the body.

Exhale as you slowly roll your spine along the floor, vertebra by vertebra. Allow your knees to drop together.

Seated Forward Fold – helps increase digestive juices and stimulates the reproductive and urinary systems.

1. Inhale as you reach your arms out to the side, and then up overhead, lengthening your spine.
2. Exhaling, bend forward from the hip joints. Do not bend at the waist. Lengthen the front of your torso. Imagine your torso coming to rest on your thighs, instead of tipping your nose toward your knees.
3. Hold onto your shins, ankles, or feet – wherever your flexibility permits.
4. Keep the front of your torso long; do not round your back. Let your belly touch your legs first, and then your chest. Your head and nose should touch your legs last.
5. With each inhalation, lengthen the front torso. With each exhalation, fold a bit deeper.
6. Hold for up to one minute. To release the pose, draw your tailbone towards the floor as you inhale and lift your torso.

Half Lord of the Fishes – every time you twist and release you are massaging your digestive organs and loosening up any trapped stools. Cleanses the internal organs.

1. Bend your right knee and tuck your right foot in near your left buttock.
2. Inhale and bring your right arm straight up beside your right ear.
3. Exhale and twist your torso to the left, bringing your right elbow to the outside of your left knee and the left palm to the floor just behind your sitting bones.
4. Take your gaze over your left shoulder, but don't strain the neck; the twist comes from your belly, not your neck.
5. On each inhale, draw the spine up tall. On each exhale, deepen the twist a little more.
6. Be sure to keep the sole of your left foot firmly planted flat on the floor.
7. Hold for 30 seconds – 1 minute.
8. When you release the pose, take a slight twist to the opposite direction as a counter pose.
9. Release the legs and switch sides.

Chapter 37
Water

THE ELIXIR OF LIFE.

We are made from water. Water carries nutrients to every cell in our body and flushes out all toxins.

We need to be well-hydrated to strengthen our immune system, keep our skin glowing and our body healthy.

Your blood consists of more than 80% water, your brain 75% and your liver a massive 96%. It is crucial you are drinking enough water daily.

Make sure when you wake up the first thing you do is drink water before you do anything else!

> **We should begin each day with around 500ml – 1 litre of fresh water on an empty stomach.**

This Will:

- Fire your metabolism up and that means weight loss.
- Keep your gut healthy (a healthy gut equals a healthy, beautiful body).
- Keeps you regular.
- Purifies your colon (again this keeps your body in tip top health). When your colon is happy you are happy.
- Hydrates you (this is so important).
- Slows aging.
- Gives your brain power.
- Gives you energy.
- Makes you eat less (drink water before you eat you might not actually be hungry).

- It flushes out all those nasty toxins lurking around your body.
- Makes your skin glow.

Studies have shown that water is so necessary to the human body that it can even cure some chronic illnesses.

Always make it your morning ritual!
DRINK 500ML – 1 litre OF WATER AS SOON AS YOU WAKE UP!

Think of water as a nutrient your body needs daily! Your health and beauty is dependent on proper hydration.

We should ideally drink when our stomach is empty from food. Drinking water with food can dilute digestive fluids, leading to poor absorption, and constipation.

I like to try and drink 3 litres a day depending on how active I am. Sometimes I squeeze in another 1.5L if I can. Always take sips, never flood yourself. Make it a habit to carry water everywhere you go.

Also add a few slices of fresh lemon to your water for clear, glowing and blemish-free skin. Lemons are powerful detoxifiers and they help to charge the water too.

Why Should You Add Lemon To Your Water?

- High vitamin C
- Detoxifying
- Helps you to produce collagen-saying goodbye to wrinkles
- Boosts energy and mood
- Alkalizing
- May heal your joints
- Regulates your bowels
- Helps metabolism
- Weight loss
- Cleanse the body and blood
- Prevents cancer

- Aids digestion – increases secretion of bile from the liver (also the cleaner your liver is the more your skin will glow)
- Flushes out bacteria and toxins in the body
- Aim to consume the juice of 2 fresh lemons each day.

You can also add a splash of sea salt to mineralise the water or add MSM powder (sulphur) for strong nails, hair and glowing skin.

Stay away from alkaline water.
It neutralizes your stomach acid and creates yeasts and fungus.
Add lemon or acv (apple cider vinegar) to your water instead.

Chapter 38
Tongue Scraping and the Gut Connection

The tongue cleaner, is a simple, thin, u-shaped piece of stainless steel. It consists of a blunted edge that removes plaque and build-up from the surface of the tongue.

The tongue cleaner prevents bad breath, especially for people who eat a lot of dairy and build up mucus in the mouth, nose, and throat. It comes from the tradition of Ayurveda, which asserts that people who use one are better at public speaking and they express themselves more thoughtfully. Some people ask if the same effect can be gained by brushing the tongue with a stiff toothbrush. Brushing the tongue moves stuff around and is helpful, but a tongue cleaner is more effective as it clears out the deep deposits and generally keeps the area cleaner, stimulated and alive.

The coating of your tongue gives you clues to your overall health as it is a reflection of the balance of bacteria in your body, the efficiency of the organs, and most importantly the function of your digestive system. Research suggests that your gut and oral health are connected. If your mouth is full of bad bacteria from eating a lot of sugar, processed foods etc., every time you swallow you are swallowing the bad bacteria too. This may then lead to a leaky gut problem also. There is also a link between bad gut health and gum disease. I had minor periodontal disease a while back and couldn't figure out why I had it because my diet is healthy and I am thorough when I clean my teeth. As soon as I stepped on the probiotic band wagon and learned I needed to heal my gut, my gums stopped bleeding. Remember, bad bacteria in the gut causes inflammation and this inflammation can show anywhere in the body. If your gums are prone to bleeding, you can also rub into your gums a drop of the essential oil myrrh. This also helps to heal any inflammation.

Here is how to do tongue scraping daily to remove excess bad bacteria from the mouth.

Directions:

- Apply a few quick strokes, 2-3 times a day, before brushing your teeth.
- Use the rounded cleaning edge to scrape gently down the tongue several times, while applying slight pressure.
- Rinse under running water and gently scrape again until no white residue is left.
- There should be no pain or gagging involved whatsoever, if you feel any discomfort, you are probably scraping too hard or starting too far back on the tongue.
- I suggest purchasing a stainless steel tongue scraper. Avoid the plastic ones. Make sure the tongue scraper is wide enough to cover the surface width of the tongue. Sometimes I also just use a tablespoon to pull the white residue out. That also works well enough if you don't have a tongue scraper.

Oil Pulling

Oil pulling is a fantastic oral detoxification procedure that is simply done by swishing a tablespoon of oil (typically coconut oil, olive or sesame oil) in your mouth for 10-20 minutes.

Oil pulling works by cleaning (detoxifying) the oral cavity in a similar way that soap cleans dirty dishes. It sucks the dirt (toxins) out of your mouth and creates a clean, antiseptic oral environment that is needed to prevent cavities and disease.

It has recently become very popular as a remedy for many different health ailments. Using this method could prevent a number of chronic illnesses.
Coconut oil is a natural antibiotic and is filled with beneficial prebiotic bacteria. Even swishing for a few seconds is beneficial. Supposedly it may even help to brighten/whiten the teeth naturally.

This method does not need to be performed daily, 3-4 times per week is sufficient.

Try adding one drop of an essential oil to coconut oil for better results such as:

- Clove
- Orange or
- Peppermint.

Chapter 39
Foods to Eat for Beauty and Health

Foods to Eat	Why
Acai Berry *or as I like to call it* **'The Beauty Berry'.** *(The highest nutrition content is in the skin).* *(High in omega-3 and omega-6).*	• Almost an identical protein and amino acid content as an egg. • Top antioxidant rich fruit. • Nourishes skin cells, supporting the creation of healthy, smooth skin. Promotes youthful and radiant skin. Great for acne sufferers. • High in vitamins B, C and E. • Rich in minerals such as potassium and calcium. • Full of fibre. • Contains high levels of essential fatty acids (omega-3 and omega-6). • Improves endurance and muscular development. • Helps with digestive health. • Helps body to rejuvenate more swiftly. • Fights cancer.

Almonds *(soak overnight to make them easier on the gut).* Eat no more than 10-12 per day.	• High in vitamin E (This helps fight the signs of aging). • Monounsaturated fats. • Zinc, calcium, iron, potassium, manganese, magnesium, selenium, copper and folate. • Full of amino acids to build protein in the body. • Known as a brain and bone food. • Known to help heal the gut but MUST be soaked.
Aloe Vera *(A* miracle food – The Healing Plant). *If you want to be beautiful all the days of your life, if you want to be flexible, have a strong immune system and nervous system then Aloe vera is for you.*	• Full of amino acids, minerals, enzymes and vitamins. • Lubricates joints, brain and nervous system. • Heals digestive illnesses like Crohn's, IBS, ulcers and colitis. Great for leaky gut. • Dissolves mucus in the intestines, which helps increase nutrient absorption. • Increases lean muscle mass. • Contains sulphur, which helps to keep your skin healthy and full of elasticity this may result in younger looking skin. • Heals inflammation in the body. It is a powerful anti-inflammatory food. • Activates the liver to produce more

	glutathione. Glutathione keeps us looking young.
	• Treats candida, parasites, fatigue, allergies, arthritis, acne and MORE.
	• Lubricates and cleans out the colon. A clean colon is needed for good health and beauty.
	• Helps every part of the body cleanse itself.
	• Helps hair growth and brings it shine back.
	• Known to heal skin cancer and other cancers too.
	• Full of natural antibiotics, minerals, enzymes and so much more.
	• This is only half of what aloe vera can do; it is God's gift.
Apples (*Be sure to buy organic so you can eat the skins for their fibre*).	• A potent food to cleanse the body. High in fibre, which cleans the colon.
	• Apple pectin is a helpful detoxifier. The pectin is also a prebiotic, which grows good bacteria.
	• They treat acne and pimples.
	• Green apples are lower in sugar than red.
	• Heal digestive disorders.
	• Helpful at boosting collagen – anti-aging.
	• Anti-inflammatory fruit.

Ashwagandha	• Provides an energetic rejuvenating lift while at the same time calming and soothing the nervous system.
(adaptogenic herb) **Ayurvedic Medicine – In India it is known as the 'Strength of the Stallion', as you may develop the strength and vitality of a horse.** The number one herb for good thyroid health.	• Relieves stress.
	• Treats exhaustion.
	• Helpful for memory, concentration and focus. Clears the mind. Known to help with Alzheimer's as well as ADHD (attention deficit disorder).
	• Boosts thyroid hormone and adrenals (*the number one herb for any thyroid issue).*
	• Helps depression.
	• Nourishes tissues.
	• Treats inflammation (e.g. arthritis, rheumatic pain). Anti-aging of the joints.
	• Helpful for infertility.
	• Improves circulation and haemoglobin.
	• Strengthens nerves.
	• Promotes sleep.
	• Lessens greying of the hair.
	• Balances hormones.
	• One of the best anti-aging herbs you can take.
	• Fights autoimmune diseases.
	• Boosts endurance and stamina. Helps to increase muscle strength and increases muscle

	mass. Great for athletes. Also promotes recovery.
	• Contains glutathione – the mother of all antioxidants.
	• Do not consume if pregnant or breast feeding.
Asparagus – *if you drink freshly pressed asparagus juice it is known to help with Rheumatoid arthritis and heals the kidneys.*	• High in potassium (reduces puffiness and bloating).
	• High in fibre, which cleanses the digestive tract and supports ongoing detoxification.
	• High in vitamin A and is a plant based source of glutathione (an antioxidant that helps mop up free radicals, great to slow down aging). Glutathione is naturally produced in the liver; it helps to also pull heavy metals out of the body such as mercury, aluminium etc. As we age we lose the ability to produce glutathione, therefore we need to eat foods rich in this antioxidant.
	• Good source of vitamin K (helps the body absorb calcium, thus proper bone formation and repair).
	• Can prevent varicose veins as rich in rutin an

	anti-inflammatory that provides circulation and strength to veins and capillaries. • Helps your skin to glow. • High in vitamin C, which helps to maintain firm skin and gives you a healthy complexion. • Helps treat UTI infections and kidney stones. A fantastic kidney food.
Astragalus (adaptogenic herb) Chinese Medicine	• Helps dry up mucus in the body. Great for candida. • Nourishes the spleen. • Boosts the immune system. • Helps with digestive health. • Gets rid of dampness in the body. • Reduces stress. • Helpful for autoimmune conditions such as fibromyalgia and more. • Boosts energy levels.
Avocados *(Have ½ an avocado a day).* Mother nature's miracle food. THE ULTIMATE GUT SOOTHER and MULTI-VITAMIN. (However, not recommended for SIBO sufferers).	• Soft, supple, skin. • Anti-aging. • Removes dead skin cells and helps to generate new skin cells, giving you a healthy glow. • Lubricates digestive tract (great for leaky gut, Crohn's, IBS etc.).

	• High in vitamins, A, C, E and K. • Loaded with beautifying minerals such as potassium, copper and iron. • Perfect anti-cellulite food. • High in amino acids (building protein in the body). A good source of the amino acid glutamine – known to help heal the gut lining. • High fibre. • Controls blood sugar – preventing you from binging on foods. • Packed with the important antioxidant Glutathione, which supports the removal of toxins from the liver. • Known as the fruit of fertility. • Eat ½ an avocado per day to help balance hormones.
Bananas *(Eat ripe bananas as these are more alkaline forming).*	• Rich in B6, which helps ward of insomnia and irritability. • May help fight depression as they boost serotonin. • High fibre and vitamin C. • May reverse IBS, and other digestive issues. • Healthy blood pressure and cholesterol levels.

	• High in calcium, potassium and magnesium. Potassium helps to moisturise the skin from within, making it look more youthful and radiant.
Baobab *(a fruit or can take in powder).*	• A rich source of vitamin C for healthy glowing skin. Vitamin C increases your absorption of iron, (baobab and moringa powder work well together). • Good for digestion. • Healthy immune system. • Increased energy. • Repairs and prevents cell damage. • A prebiotic – high in fibre. • High in antioxidants. • Full of calcium. • Known as 'The Tree of Life'.
Barley Grass	• Detoxifies the liver. • Protects against cancer. • Treats ulcerative colitis. • Boosts immune system. • Anti-inflammatory. • Delays aging. • Removes toxins / cleans blood. • High in chlorophyll. • Rich in calcium. • Rich in beauty enzymes.
Bee Pollen *(Avoid if any known bee*	• High in potassium (reduces puffiness and

allergies). **HIGH PROTEIN FOOD.** *Take 1 tbsp. a day in smoothies or off the spoon.* **I would consider this as one of my TOP beauty foods.**	bloating). Over flowing with vitamins, minerals and enzymes. • Great for healing your body from within. • Will enhance your glow, beauty and energy. • Known to rejuvenate the body and lengthen life. • Increases brain power. • Fights acne, depression and improves digestion. • Known to help improve fertility and libido. • Filled with B vitamins and B12; however it's not known if the body can manufacture it. • Provides stress relief, balances hormones and also cleans toxins from the body. • High levels of collagen repairing vitamin C and vitamin E, making it a potent anti-aging, anti-wrinkle food. • Ingesting these nutrients provide an internal form of sun protection. • Complete protein. 22 full amino acids. • Balances cravings. • High in calcium iron, potassium and zinc. • High in those beauty enzymes, which help with digestion.

	• Increases stamina, energy and immunity. • World class athletes use it.
Bee Propolis *(propolis is sometimes in bee pollen – the dark granules).* *It's what bees coat their beehives with to protect the hive from harmful bacteria.* Anything from the bee is generally considered to be a magical healing food. We really do need to save the bees.	• A very powerful anti-viral, anti-biotic, anti-bacterial. • Fights against pneumonia and ulcers. • Can speed up healing of broken bones. • Fights cavities, gum disease, high blood pressure, skin cancer, and everything else. It's powerful stuff. • A rich source of minerals, amino acids, fats, vitamin C and E. • Treats parasites – may help to eliminate them.
Beetroot *(Use the green tops if you have them from the farmer's market. Beet greens are one of the best sources for chlorophyll, iron, potassium and vitamins A and C).* **Juice recipe to fight wrinkles:** • **1 beetroot** • **2 carrots** • **4-6 kale leaves** • **1 green apple**	• Stimulates liver function. • Helps oxygenate the blood. Powerful blood builder and cleanser, removing toxins and congestion from the body. • Rich in antioxidants. Great for an overly acidic body. • Detoxifying. Purifies the blood of toxins. • High in Iodine, which is needed for good thyroid health. • Helps with muscle development.

• **½ lemon** If you take beetroot regularly, apparently you will look younger.	• Rich in minerals calcium, magnesium and potassium, fibre and iron. • Full of B vitamins. • High in vitamins C and A. • Prevents the skin from premature aging; helping to maintain a youthful, glowing appearance. • Keeps the skin firm. • They brighten your eyes and help to make them glow. • Great for endurance runners to give you energy. The nitrates in beet juice boost stamina. They also reduce inflammation in athletes. • When consumed regularly, can help prevent varicose veins.
Blueberries (look for wild blueberries they are more nutritious). **Juice recipe to stop aging:** • **2 red apples** • **½ lemon or lime** • **2 cups blueberries** • **Fresh coconut water.**	• Known to give you beautiful skin. • Strengthen eyes and vision. • Contain vitamins A, C and E. • Rich in minerals, selenium, magnesium, calcium, zinc, copper, iron and phosphorous. • High in B vitamins for energy. • A good source of fibre. • Known to contain compounds that increase

	• beneficial bacteria in the gut. • A low sugar fruit.
Brazil Nuts *(only 2–4 is enough to eat daily). Put in salads/smoothies or add to foods.*	• They contain selenium, which protects the skin from cell damage. • Needed for thyroid and gut health.
Broccoli	• A TOP beauty food. • Nourishes the skin, joints and connective tissue around the body to help you move more fluidly. • High in calcium, magnesium and zinc. • Helps keep your bones strong and keeps your body more alkaline. • High in folate and iron; which keeps the blood healthy. • Contains vitamin A and C, which has collagen smoothing repairing properties. Fabulous anti-aging benefits. • Try to eat the stems or juice them too. • Broccoli sprouts are even better as mentioned in the 'Sprouts' chapter.
Brussels Sprouts	• High sulphur. Great for skin health and gut health. • Excellent source of vitamins A, C and E. • They contain vitamin K, keeping joints healthy so you can move gracefully.

	• They contain omega-3 fatty acids. Needed for beautiful, moisturised skin. • Are a great source of calcium, potassium and folate. • High in fibre. • Can help lower cholesterol. • Anti-inflammatory food – known to help lower inflammation in the intestines.
Buckwheat *(Find buckwheat flour, soba noodles, pasta etc., this is gluten free.) Actually comes from the rhubarb family.*	• A complete protein contains all essential amino acids and essential fatty acids. • Helpful in repairing collagen. • High in fibre. • High in many of the B vitamins as well as phosphorous, magnesium, iron, folate, zinc, copper and manganese. • A complex whole grain, great for diabetics to stabilize blood sugar. • Can also help to lower blood pressure and cholesterol.
Burdock Root	• Important for acne as it supports the liver. • Rich in iron for healthy hair.
Cabbage (Raw)	• Stimulates the immune system.

	<ul><li>Kills bacteria and viruses.</li><li>Heals ulcers.</li><li>A miracle cleanser and healer.</li><li>Great for acne sufferers.</li></ul>
Cacao *(Raw Chocolate)* You know I'm a BIG raw chocolate fan – **THE BEST ANTI-AGING / GUT HEALING FOOD.**	<ul><li>Supports a healthy cardiovascular system.</li><li>High source of magnesium – this means veins and arteries can relax, improving the flow of blood, oxygen, and nutrients throughout the body. Magnesium also helps with the elasticity of the skin, promoting youthful skin and tissues.</li><li>High in iron – iron is part of the oxygen-carrying protein called haemoglobin that keeps our blood healthy.</li><li>Rich in serotonin. Serotonin is what boosts your mood and helps diminish anxiety. Great for stress.</li><li>Good source of zinc for beautiful skin and hair.</li><li>Known to be a great anti-aging food as high in polyphenols. These polyphenols also help to break down fat in cellulite. YES! An anti-cellulite / anti-aging food and it is CHOCOLATE!</li></ul>

Camu Camu Berry (High in vitamin C). Vitamin C is required for the synthesis of collagen in our bodies.	• Contains the world's **highest vitamin C content.** • Excellent source of calcium, phosphorous, potassium, and iron. • Supports the immune system, maintains excellent eyesight, creates beautiful skin, supports strong collagen, decreases inflammation, improves lung health and helps with stress and anxiety. • Another beauty berry.
Carrots	• Good eye health. • Create gorgeous hair. • Gets rid of oily skin, combats wrinkles and leaves your skin moisturised from the inside out. Strong anti-aging properties. • High amount of beta-carotene, which converts into vitamin A, needed for a healthy scalp, which is essential for healthy hair growth. • Strong cleansing properties. Detoxifying the liver, helping to remove toxins from the blood. • Contain calcium, potassium, iron, fibre, vitamins B1, B2, B6, C, K and biotin.

	• Make your skin glow. • Promote collagen. • Good for health of spleen, stomach and kidneys. • Drinking fresh raw carrot juice is also known to heal the GI tract (small intestine).
Celery *(Try to have the leaves attached to the stems. They have a high concentration of vitamin A).* ***Tip:*** *Drink celery juice straight after the gym to re-hydrate and make it the base of every juice you make every day.*	• Potassium and sodium can flush out excess bodily fluids, which can help reduce puffiness throughout the body. • Anti-inflammatory food. • Has a calming effect on the nervous system. • Contains minerals such as calcium, magnesium, folate, iron and potassium. • Helps lower blood pressure. • Reduces stress hormones (cortisol). • Can help skin around the eyes look healthier, reducing puffy eyes. • Greatly improves appearance. • Eliminates toxins from the body. • A natural laxative. • Excellent source of B2, B6 and C. • Helps prevent ulcers. Celery contains a special type of ethanol extract that is useful in

	protecting the lining of the digestive tract from ulcers. Known to help heal a leaky gut.
Chia Seeds *(Make you lean and strong). The gel helps you stay full for hours. (Good source of omega-3 and omega-6).* Contain more omega-3 than salmon.	• An important food to maintain the tone of the body and good health. • Increase stamina and endurance. Excellent workout food. • Balance blood sugar levels. Keep your energy steady for hours and throughout your workout. Also help to replace amino acids after a workout. • Complete protein. Contains ALL essential amino acids to repair the muscle tissue in your body, keeping you looking more toned as well as raising energy levels. • Help with ongoing cleansing as they keep your colon hydrated, making sure foods pass easily through your system, so that waste, which can end up being stored as fat cells, is reduced. • Good source of omega-3 fatty acids. Balance hormones and nerve functions. Anti-inflammatory.

	<ul><li>High in antioxidants, which help eliminate aging free radicals.</li><li>High in calcium, magnesium, and boron.</li><li>Clean your heart, colon and arteries.</li><li>They are very hydrating.</li><li>The Aztecs used chia to relieve joint pain and help with skin conditions.</li><li>A great internal cleanser.</li></ul>
Chicory Root **Note: If you have SIBO or IBS, this maybe best to avoid.**	<ul><li>Contains inulin, a soluble fibre that feeds digestive flora in the intestines. A great prebiotic.</li><li>May provide direct support to the digestive system but causes SIBO to flare up.</li></ul>
Coriander (cilantro) and Parsley	<ul><li>Both remove heavy metals from the body.</li><li>**Coriander** – removes mercury from the body.</li><li>**Parsley** – detoxifier and diuretic, helping to prevent bloating and water retention by flushing out the kidneys.</li><li>Both great for the lungs.</li><li>Parsley helps oxygen metabolism.</li><li>Aid digestion, clean the blood and purify.</li><li>Rich in vitamins A, C and E, plus most minerals.</li><li>A great anti-cellulite food.</li></ul>

	• High in folate and iron, to maintain a healthy glow. • Chewing parsley is great for bad breath. • Parsley kills bacteria in the body and helps to rejuvenate the liver. A great superfood. Known as a multi-vitamin, it gives your body everything it needs.
Cinnamon	• High in antioxidants reducing the formation of free radicals. • Helps to repair damage to all parts of your body, from skin to organs. • Anti-inflammatory – heals the gut. • Boosts metabolism and reduces hunger pains as well as sugar cravings. • Boosts circulation, which helps to give you a healthy glow. Anti-aging.
Coconut *(Coconuts can save your life).* Coconut cannot be stored in the body as fat; it actually needs to be burned up on the spot. **Nutrition Tip:** *When you buy coconut milk, DO NOT get reduced fat, many of the good*	• Best natural hydrators. • Young coconut water is identical to human blood plasma. • High in Lauric acid, iron, potassium, magnesium and calcium. • Young coconut meat has healing and youth promoting qualities. • Provide energy. • Can help normalise blood sugar levels.

health properties are due to its medium-chain triglycerides, which are easier to burn for energy than to store as fat. These MCT's are needed for beautiful skin and good health. The MCT's are not available in the low fat varieties.	• Support healthy hormone production. • Anti-bacterial (helps destroy yeast and fungi, great for candida, acne, psoriasis etc.). • Support thyroid function. • Speed up metabolism. • Give the face a lift and reduce bags under the eyes. • Coconut oil rubbed into skin prevents stretch marks. • The MCT's in coconut oil have also been shown to reverse early stages of Alzheimer's.
Collard Greens *(replace wheat wraps etc. with these instead).*	• They brighten your skin. • They fight under eye circles and discoloration. • Rich in minerals, calcium, iron, potassium, magnesium. • Rich in vitamins K, C and E. • Also contain beta-carotene and lutein to maintain eye health. This also decreases the risk of wrinkles. Beta-carotene is needed for good skin health. • They help to ease stress as high in magnesium. Magnesium relaxes the body. • Can eliminate toxins from the body.

	• FULL of CHLOROPHYLL, which means glowing skin!
Cucumbers *(One of the most healing fruits on Earth). Amazing for your skin and hair.* **Beauty Juice:** **6 celery ribs** **1 green apple** **4 small cucumbers.** **Place through a cold pressed juicer.**	• High in enzyme charged water. • Full of B vitamins. • High in potassium, calcium, iron and magnesium. • The mineral silica is found in abundance in cucumbers. This is essential for a glowing, youthful complexion. • The flesh of cucumbers is high in vitamin C. (Buy organic to eat the skins). • They flush out the body and prevent bloating. • They detoxify the body; clean the bowels, and the gut. • The best kidney cleanser (great for dark circles and puffy eyes).
Dandelions *(buy the root or in tea).*	• A SUPERFOOD. • High in vitamins A, E, C, and D. • Minerals – calcium, iron, manganese, magnesium, phosphorous, potassium, sulphur, silicon, sodium and more. • Clean blood. • Help digestive system. • Remove acid from the blood.

	- Cleanse and support the liver. - Great for healthy hair. - Known to help fight cancer. - Treats acne and other skin conditions.
Durians – A fruit from Thailand. *(Apparently they make you more beautiful but they do smell bad).*	- High in protein. Excellent muscle builder. - A good food for depression and insomnia as high in tryptophan. They raise brain serotonin, which is made in the gut and therefore they make you feel happy. - Strong blood cleansers. - High in vitamin E. Anti-aging.
Dulse *(add to salads, good replacement for salt as natural salty taste).* **(Contain at least 50% protein).**	- Nourishes your body and hair follicle with vitamins B6, B12, E and A, rich in iron, zinc, calcium, potassium and magnesium as well as iodine, which is needed for a healthy thyroid. - Look for whole dulse leaves, the dulse flakes can be a fishy taste. - Known to help pull heavy metals out of the body such as lead, mercury etc. Needed for anyone with an autoimmune concern. - The secret to glowing skin and lustrous locks is

	found in seaweed rich foods.
Fennel	• Great for puffy, oily (acne prone) or wrinkled skin. • Helpful also to reduce fine lines.
Flaxseeds *(Ground flaxseeds are a great source of omega-3. Take 1tbsp. – 2bsp. per day off the spoon or add to smoothie, meals etc.)*	• Vitamin B6, calcium, magnesium, folate, iron, zinc, manganese. • High fibre. • Stabilize blood sugar levels. • Promote internal cleansing. • Omega-3 fatty acids. Anti-inflammatory – needed for healthy/plump skin. • Best stored in the fridge as they can go rancid quickly. • A great food to balance hormones.
Figs *(Contain one of the highest concentrations of calcium).*	• The seeds cleanse the digestive tract of toxins and mucus. • One of nature's best laxatives. • Top mucus dissolving food.
Garlic	• Purifies the blood stream, enhances detoxification. • Optimises digestion. • A natural deterrent to internal yeast infections. Great for candida.

	• Supports the cardiovascular system.
	• Packed with vitamins and nutrients, including potassium, B vitamins and vitamin C.
	• Supports the immune system.
	• A wonderful natural antibiotic. Nature's medicine. You should aim to eat 1 raw garlic clove daily to keep your immune system strong.
	• Anti-inflammatory.
	• High in sulphur, which can help to heal the gut and also creates beautiful skin and hair.
Ginger	• Age-defying antioxidant, high in vitamin C.
	• Increases blood circulation to the scalp and the skin, which minimizes age spots, evens out skin tones, fights wrinkles, shedding off years.
	• Great for digestion, which helps eliminate bloating and speeds up the removal of beauty robbing toxins.
	• It can reduce acne and improve the shine to your hair.
	• Also great for boosting your immune system.
	• Anti-inflammatory.

	• Another natural antibiotic. Try to consume a little every day.
Ginseng **Adaptogenic Herb**	• Energy boost. • Great pre-workout. • Boosts immune system. • Treats cancer, heart disease and menopausal symptoms. • Helps to balance hormones. Also great for thyroid health.
Goji Berries – **The Fountain of** **Youth.** *Nicknamed the longevity fruit.* *They keep skin plump and healthy.*	• Boost immune function. • They boost the natural production of growth hormone, which helps us stay young and boost our metabolism. They are the only known food that boost HGH (human growth hormone). • Are a rich source of l-glutamine and l-arginine, which is needed for leaky gut. • They have a calming effect on digestion. • Anti-inflammatory food. • Balance blood sugar levels *(great if you are fighting a sugar addiction. Eat a handful every day).* • Cancer fighting properties. • Improve vison. • Have more beta-carotene than carrots.

	• A complete protein source on par with bee pollen. • Contain over 21 trace minerals such as zinc, iron, copper, calcium, selenium, and phosphorous. All needed for beautiful skin and good gut health. • Vitamin B1, B6, and vitamin E.
Grapefruit	• Flushes out toxins. • Keeps skin cells strong and balanced. • The oils in grapefruits are fat dissolvers that will help reduce cellulite. Support the lymphatic system. • They remove excess water and promote a smoother skin appearance. • Helps detoxify, very cleansing to the liver.
Gotu kola	• Anti-aging, rejuvenating herb. • Known as the 'fountain of youth', and is said to preserve the mind, as well as the body. • Stimulates collagen production. More collagen means skin with more elasticity, bounciness, and firmness, i.e. less wrinkles.

Hemp Seeds (Contain omega-3, omega-6 and omega-9).	• Long, lean, muscle tone. High in plant protein. Contain ALL amino acids and essential fatty acids to maintain human life.
	• A SUPER SEED, loaded with phytonutrients to nourish healthy blood, tissues, cells, and organs that make for a beautiful, toned body.
	• They help the body burn excess fat and remove toxins from the skin, intestinal tract, kidneys and lungs.
	• High in minerals zinc, calcium, magnesium, sulphur, copper, iodine, chromium, iron and more.
	• Contain omega-6 fats, which can help support a healthy metabolism and fat burning functions.
	• Balance hormones. Supports progesterone levels (the sex hormone, needed for beautiful skin and to balance out oestrogen).
	• Anti-inflammatory.
	• Also contain omega-9, which is considered to be a beautifying oil.
	• Hempseed is one of the few seeds that also contain chlorophyll.

	• Known to potentially be a source of vitamin D.
Holy Basil or Tulsi (Ayurvedic Herb)	• Helps balance ALL of your hormones. • Great for PCOS, PMS and menopause. • Anti-inflammatory. • Boosts energy and focus. • Helps with adrenal and thyroid health. Relieves stress. • Controls acne breakouts as it purifies the blood. • Fights cancer. • Helpful for autoimmune conditions. • Slows down aging. • Treats eczema.
Kale (*Think toned and lean when you see the name kale*). *Kale and all greens make you LEAN!*	• Strengthening food. • Improves skins firmness and suppleness. • Contains large amounts of manganese, iron, copper and calcium. • Battles free radicals and cellular oxidation by supplying huge amounts of powerful antioxidants. • Keeps your body strong and resilient. • High levels of vitamin C and A. Reverses aging and sun damage. • One cup of kale provides about 10% of the recommended daily allowance of omega-3 fatty acids, which helps

	regulate hormones in your body. • Anti-inflammatory, protecting against stiff joints and arthritis. • Prevents hair breakage and nails chipping. • High in vitamin K, working well with calcium to build strong bones. Vitamin K is also a beauty enhancer. *A powerful beauty food.* • High in fibre. • Great for detoxification. Kale encourages the liver to produce enzymes that detoxify cancer-causing chemicals. • High in chlorophyll – blood builder. Remember, the cleaner our blood, the more beautiful and healthy we are. • They say kale has more protein than beef.
Kiwi – Top Beauty Fruit.	• Prevent free radicals from damaging the skin, slow down the signs of aging and stimulates the production of collagen. • Rich in essential fatty acids and vitamin E and C. • They help eliminate fine lines, dark circles and a dull complexion.

	• Also contain omega-3 oils in the seeds – anti-inflammatory.
Lemon *(Drink warm water with lemon each morning. Aim to have 2 lemons per day).* Apparently if you drink lemon juice every day for 3 months you can rejuvenate the liver back to new. Lemons and limes both have similar beauty and health benefits.	• Clear, glowing and blemish free skin. • Repairs damaged skin cells. • Regular intake of lemon water can cure acne, blackheads and other skin infections. • High in vitamin C. • Purifies the blood. • Flushes out bacteria and toxins in the body. • Aids digestion, helping with weight loss. • Alkaline forming. • Fights wrinkles and rejuvenates the skin from within. • Contains, calcium, potassium and magnesium. • An amazing cleanser. • Rejuvenates liver tissue.
Liquorice Root (Adaptogenic herb)	• Supports stomach and digestion. Helps to heal a leaky gut. • Lowers stress – heals ulcers in the stomach due to stress. • Supports small intestinal health. Helpful for autoimmune conditions.
Manuka Honey	• Helps with SIBO, low stomach acid and acid reflux.

	• Known to help with IBS. • Balances your digestive system to heal stomach and intestinal imbalances. • A natural antibiotic. • Anti-microbial and healing properties. • Boosts immune system. • Boosts vitality, energy and has been known to improve skin tone and texture. • Helps to promote restful sleep.
Maca *(Buy in powder form).* *Is a member of the cruciferous family, broccoli, cauliflower, kale etc.*	• Keeps your hormones in check. Adaptogenic. • Increases energy, endurance, oxygen in the blood, and it supports the adrenals, and the thyroid. • Helps to boost mood. • Rich in calcium, magnesium, phosphorous, potassium, sulphur, sodium and iron. Contains zinc, iodine, copper, selenium. • Also rich in vitamins B1, B2, C and E. • Known to help deal with stress. • Helps to increase fertility and libido. • Is a powerful strength and stamina enhancer. Great for athletes. • Is known to help improve the following conditions:

	chronic fatigue, depression, lack of libido, poor memory, stress, tension and malnutrition.
	• Boosts the shine of your hair and strengthens nails.
	• Anti-aging.
	• Works well with cacao powder.
Macadamia nuts	• High in selenium and the beauty mineral zinc.
	• Contain the beautifying mono-unsaturated fat called oleic acid.
	• They help the body efficiently burn fat.
Matcha Tea or Green Tea	• Increases energy.
	• Prevents cancer.
	• Detoxifies. Removes heavy metals and chemicals from the body.
	• Enhances mood.
	• Improves skin.
	• Boosts immune system.
	• Boosts memory and concentration.
	• Burns calories. Helpful for weight loss.
	• Combats inflammation, oxidation and aging.
	• High chlorophyll content.
	• Increases calmness and reduces stress.
	• Powerful antibiotic and anti-viral.

	• Known to also heal a leaky gut as anti-inflammatory.
Medicinal Mushrooms *(Reishi/Cordyceps/ Maitake/Chaga).* Reishi is known as The Mushroom of Immortality as it extends life. Supports anti-aging.	• Boost the immune system. • Help fight viruses such as candida. • Destroy tumour and cancer cells. • Detoxify chemicals and heavy metals out of the body (lead, mercury, aluminium etc.). Needed for autoimmune conditions. • Balance cortisol levels and other hormones. Helpful for PMS, menopause, PMT, PCOS and infertility issues. • Supply beneficial microbes with prebiotics, to keep them well fed. Good for the gut. • Energise your body. • Anti-aging. • Anti-inflammatory.
Millet – gluten free	• Alkaline forming in the body. Anti-inflammatory. • Easily digested by almost everyone. • Plant based protein with complex carbohydrates. • Good source of B1, which supports muscles and a healthy nervous system.

	• The phosphorous in millet aids with fat metabolism, body tissue repair and the creation of energy. • Packed with fibre. • An all-round power food. • Contains minerals calcium, manganese, tryptophan *(for serotonin production, which helps to calm and soothe the nerves)*, phosphorous, most of the B vitamins, vitamins E and K, iron, zinc, copper and omega-3 fatty acids.
Moringa *(leaf or powder).* Packed with calcium.	• Rich in proteins and contains minerals such as magnesium, calcium, iron, zinc and potassium. • High in vitamins A, E, B3, and B2. All essential for beautiful hair and skin. • Delays aging process. • Boosts stamina and endurance. • Helps with thyroid. • Fights dark circles under the eyes. • Treats depression. • Anti-inflammatory. • Accelerates growth of new skin cells. • Increases energy.

MSM (Sulphur) The Beauty Mineral. *This is an organic compound that is naturally derived from the earth's rain cycle. It is one of the most critical nutrients for our bodies to remain youthful and energetic.*	• Treats osteoarthritis and joint pain. Improving joint flexibility, skin and muscle tissue. • Helps to heal a leaky gut and other digestive issues. • Restores hair growth – helping to give you long, lustrous locks. • Treats skin issues such as acne. • Helps you to remain youthful and energetic as it is necessary for collagen production. MSM works well with vitamin C. • Detoxifies the body – helps to pull heavy metals out such as mercury etc. Another help for autoimmune conditions. • Accelerates healing. • Anti-inflammatory – helping to heal any chronic inflammation in the body.
Nettle Tea	• Anti-inflammatory – can help relieve symptoms of acne, eczema and other blemishes you may have. • The antioxidants contained in the tea can also help speed healing and prevent scarring on the skin. • Boosts immune system.

	<ul><li>Destroys parasites.</li><li>Helps your hair health, making it strong and long. Good for hair loss.</li><li>Builds blood, very cleansing.</li><li>Rich in vitamins and minerals.</li><li>A natural beauty remedy for skin and hair.</li></ul>
Noni juice or fruit *(A miracle fruit that can help you live longer).*	<ul><li>Aids in weight loss – helps to metabolize a lot of energy.</li><li>Good for digestion – high fibre content.</li><li>Anti-inflammatory, relieving pain and chronic inflammation.</li><li>Anti-cancer properties.</li><li>Boosts immunity.</li><li>Increases energy levels.</li><li>Prevents stomach ulcers.</li><li>A rich source of vitamin C. Treats skin problems such as acne etc. and slows aging. Preserves the skins elasticity. Known to help your skin glow from the inside out.</li><li>Combats hair loss. High in vitamins and minerals.</li></ul>
Nutritional Yeast *(This is gluten free).* **Look for nutritional yeast with added B12.**	<ul><li>High in amino acids (protein) and B vitamins.</li><li>Contains 15 key minerals, such as zinc, selenium, magnesium, manganese and copper.</li></ul>

	• Gives energy to your body's cells. • Keeps your hair colour strong and your hair shiny and healthy. • High in fibre. • Contains chromium, which balances blood sugar levels *(needed for sugar cravings)*.
Oats – look for gluten free, whole-grain rolled organic oats. *Avoid oats that are quick and easy; these are processed and will cause a rise in blood sugar. They may also cause inflammation in the gut.*	• Vitamin E, B and other vital vitamins plus minerals calcium, magnesium, potassium, selenium, copper, zinc, iron and manganese. • High fibre. Great for your colon health. • Beneficial to heart health, lower blood pressure and can even help prevent diabetes.
Olives and Olive Oil – Always take in RAW. DO NOT HEAT! (If heated, this may inflame the tissues and accelerate aging, destroying your complexion and could lead to acne). **Fact:** *Green olives are actually unripe, picked early from the tree. At this stage the fruit has not set its full oil and mineral content.*	• The most beautifying foods of all. Slows down the aging process. • High source of vitamin E. (Vitamin E is known to erase fine lines on the face, repair connective tissue, heal the circulatory system, and soothe the digestive system. • Olives are anti-fungal and anti-bacterial. • Loaded with omega-3 and omega-6 fatty acids. • High in vitamin A.

Look for organic cold pressed in a dark glass bottle. They are light sensitive and also avoid all in plastic bottles. This makes them toxic.	• Lubricates the joints. • I like to use olive oil in the bath and I also use it to shave my legs with. It is a natural moisturiser for dry skin and will leave your skin silky soft. • Heals damaged skin.
Onions *(Contain quercetin, which heals the gut.)*	• Cleanse the liver and skin. • Antibacterial, balances bad bacteria in the body. • Full of sulphuric oils, which stimulate the digestive tract. These oils prevent purification in the intestines. A healer to the gut. Sulphur also slows aging down in the body and prevents and heals inflammation of the joints. • Blood cleanser. • Vitamins A and C, calcium, potassium, iron, silicon and fibre.
Papaya *(Eating them often will help make your skin and hair's lustre improve and make your skin more beautiful, also helping to brighten eyes).* **Try to eat one every day and see how you feel and look!**	• High in the enzyme papain, which is similar to the stomach enzyme pepsin. Great for your digestive system. • Cleans old debris from the inside out and allows all nutrients to reach all areas of the body. • Papaya oxygenates the body and cleanses the tissues. • Helps alleviate gas.

Note – do not eat if wishing to conceive, they are known to be a natural contraception for male and female.	• The enzymes help protect against wrinkles. • Cleanses the digestive tract and promotes digestion. Great for inflamed bowels. • Have anti-tumour and anti-cancer properties. • Contain high concentrations of vitamins A and C, which repair the skin and keep it youthful. • They tighten skin. • Helps to get rid of parasites *(especially when you eat the seeds).* The seeds can be added to a salad dressing for a peppery kick.
Pears *(Buy organic to eat the skins).*	• Support lungs and colon. • Useful in treating inflammatory conditions. • Protect against developing asthma. • Colon cleansing food. Cleans the digestive tract of aging toxins and wastes. A good fruit for autoimmune conditions. • Vitamins C, E and some B vitamins and vitamin K. • Copper, manganese, potassium, iron, magnesium, selenium, calcium, zinc and folate.

Pineapple *(packed with the enzyme bromelain).*	• Great for digestion. • High in the enzyme bromelain (this breaks down protein and foods through your system, and cleanses the blood by removing debris and toxins from the bloodstream). It also helps improve circulation and reduces mucus. A wonderful fruit for good gut health. • Reduces gas, anti-bloating food. • Anti-inflammatory. • High in vitamin C, manganese *(this regulates blood sugar levels).* • Known to be a beautifying fruit as they promote glowing skin. • May stimulate collagen production. Anti-aging.
Pine Nuts	• Contain more protein than any other nut or seed. • High in fibre, zinc, MSM (sulphur), iron and essential fatty acids. • Great for aging and inflammation. • High in healthy fats. • Great for energy. • Good for joint health.
Pumpkin Seeds *(Packed with omega-3 and*	• Excellent source of zinc, sulphur and vitamin A (all help build strong

omega-6). ***Anti-aging.***	hair). Zinc in pumpkin seeds maintains collagen. • Promotes skin renewal for a radiant and healthier complexion. • Help with dark circles under the eyes. • Ward off acne and other skin imbalances – helping to produce clear, radiant skin. • Kill off parasites in the gut. • Contain B vitamins, which include biotin, an essential nutrient for strengthening hair, increasing hair growth. TOP hair building food. Great for men dealing with baldness. • Rich source of essential fatty acids, which nourish the scalp. • High in vitamins C, E, K and A. • Supply a good amount of protein, magnesium, calcium, phosphorous, manganese, copper and iron, all build a healthy blood flow. • A good seed to help balance hormones.
Quinoa – *have cooked or raw veggies along with it. Try to only consume 2-3x per week max.*	• Necessary for building muscle and a toned body. • Complete plant protein. Contains ALL essential amino acids the body

	requires as the building blocks for muscle. <ul><li>Tissue growth and repair.</li><li>High in minerals, copper and manganese, as well as magnesium, which helps to relax the blood vessels and muscles.</li><li>Rich in fibre, which helps ensure elimination of toxins and keeps your digestive tract cleansed.</li></ul>
Radishes – repair the gut. **Also a TOP BEAUTY FOOD.**	<ul><li>Hair strengthening food.</li><li>High in vitamin C as well as silicon and sulphur.</li><li>Top mucus dissolving food. Dissolves mucus in the digestive tract, so nutrients can flow freely.</li><li>Cleanse and detoxify the body. The cleaner the body, the healthier the hair.</li><li>Used in Russia to treat hyperthyroidism as they help to keep levels of thyroid hormones in balance.</li></ul>
Raw Apple Cider Vinegar (*unfiltered, contains 'The Mother'*). *Good for cleansing the body from the inside out.* **Take 2 tablespoons every morning in water or add to salads and other**	<ul><li>Natural antidote for acne.</li><li>Strong digestive aid.</li><li>Antiviral, antibacterial and antifungal properties, *(helpful with candida and yeast issues).*</li><li>Flushes out toxins and stress hormones.</li><li>Relieves water retention around the thighs and stomach.</li></ul>

recipes. Begin with 1 tsp. if new to ACV. **Recipe:** *2 heaped tsp. of raw honey or Manuka honey with 2 tsp. of ACV. Fill the glass with water and sip slowly. Rich in potassium, which combats chronic fatigue. Renews vitality and stiffness.*	• Promotes the growth of probiotics (the beneficial bacteria in your body), for a healthy digestive system. • Contains potassium, enzymes and other trace minerals. • May help alleviate sugar cravings. • Speeds up metabolism and encourages fat burning. A good cellulite food. • You can maintain youthful looking skin by taking this every day. • Relieves chronic fatigue. • ACV keeps you more youthful, healthier, stronger, flexible and trim.
Raw Honey – A great alternative to have instead of sugar.	• A natural occurring anti-biotic and antiseptic. • An essential natural CURE-ALL. • Fights bacteria, blocks infection, combats inflammation, reduces pain, improves circulation, stimulates growth of tissue, reduces scarring and makes healing faster. • Full of every vitamin, mineral and enzyme your body needs. • If you apply to your skin it is known for its anti-

	aging benefits as well as zaps acne. Supposedly gives you your glow back.
Red Bell Peppers	• High in vitamin C (repairs and regenerates collagen). • Low in sugar. • High in silicon, which diminishes wrinkles and makes skin more supple and youthful. • Try to buy organic – a dirty dozen food.
Rocket (Arugula) A GLOW FOOD.	• High in vitamins A, C and K (protecting skin from free radicals and helping with acne). • Highly alkaline. • Helps cleanse and neutralise acidic waste through the blood and lymphatic system. • High in iron, calcium and fibre. • Protects skin from sun damage *(eat your suntan from the inside out)*.
Romaine Lettuce	• Rich in nutrients. • High in vitamin C and beta-carotene. • Rich source of folate and potassium, which helps regulate blood pressure. • A good source of iron, rich in vitamin K, manganese, vitamins B1, B2, and chromium *(good*

	for stabilising blood sugar).
Royal Jelly (The fountain of youth and beauty).	• It is rejuvenating and regenerating for the body. • Slows aging, maintains skin tone, promotes sexual vitality, alleviates arthritis pain and acts as an anti-depressant. • Known to help those suffering from Alzheimer's. Great for memory. • A powerful energy supplement. • Contains B5 and other B vitamins plus amino acids, potassium, magnesium, calcium, zinc and iron.
Schizandra Berry Chinese Medicine (Adaptogenic Herb)	• Helps with dark circles under the eyes *(this is usually a sign of adrenal burnout).* • Supports liver, kidneys and adrenal health. Also the thyroid as the adrenals and thyroid are usually connected. • Known to beautify the skin. • They nourish your overall body. • Help to balance hormones.
Seaweed *(Try to have every day).*	• Binds with heavy metals (like mercury) and removes them out of your

	body. Another great food for autoimmune conditions.
	• More iron than spinach. Iron is needed for healthy, glowing skin.
	• Makes your hair grow faster. Can even turn grey hair dark again – apparently.
	• You can add to the blender with pineapple.
	• Best source of natural iodine for healthy thyroids.
	• Contains almost all beauty minerals we need.
	• High in amino acids for protein.
	• Anti-inflammatory, anti-microbial, anti-fungal and anti-cancer.
	• Loaded with calcium.
	• Fights candida.
	• Makes you look younger.
	• Rich in fibre.
	• EAT EVERYDAY!
Sesame Seeds and Tahini	• High in iron, zinc, magnesium, manganese and copper.
	• Good source of B vitamins.
	• Anti-inflammatory.
	• Good source of high-quality dietary protein.

Spinach	<ul><li>Rich in beta-carotene which, converts to vitamin A (anti-aging). Vitamin A is also needed for a healthy gut.</li><li>Contains the antioxidant alpha lipoic acid, which helps with conditions such as acne, rosacea, skin aging, Alzheimer's and diabetes.</li><li>Contains vitamins C, E and K.</li><li>High in the minerals manganese, calcium, magnesium, zinc, iron, folate and selenium.</li><li>High in amino acids, which are needed for a strong body.</li><li>Packed with fibre. Great for colon health.</li><li>Gives you your glow back.</li></ul>
Spirulina and Chlorella – green algae's. *(Full of friendly flora that optimises nutrient absorption and increase immunity. Great for gut health).* **Have one of them every day (rotate). Take 1 tsp. – 1 tbsp. per day.** *I have both every day; you can*	<ul><li>Oxygenating and alkalizing properties.</li><li>Increase cellular regeneration and create a healthy, beautiful glow.</li></ul> **Spirulina** <ul><li>Around 60% protein. A builder of lean muscle.</li><li>Rich source of iron. Contains as much iron as meat.</li><li>Good source of vitamin B complex, D and K.</li><li>Rich in magnesium and trace minerals.</li></ul>

also do that if you wish.	• Possess potent detoxifying properties and can cleanse mercury and other heavy metals and toxins from the body. Again good for autoimmune diseases. • High concentrations of chlorophyll – blood builder. • Rich in antioxidants, fighting free radicals that can damage your cells. • Helps with stamina and endurance. Great for athletes or demanding workouts. *My go to work out food. ALWAYS!* • Can help curb hunger. • Cleanses and helps to suppress the overgrowth of bad bacteria like candida. • Regular consumption can help stimulate immunity and wound healing. • Balances hormones. • Dissolves fat deposits – helpful for weight loss. • Prevents heart problems and reduces cholesterol. • Rich in the essential fatty acid gamma-linolenic acid (GLA), which is needed for gorgeous skin and strong, shiny hair. • Fights inflammation. • High in sulphur (beauty mineral) – improves

	physical strength, flexibility, agility, skin health, speed of healing, hair lustre and helps to rid our tissues of toxins. *I can't live without spirulina.*
	Chlorella
	• Considered to be one of the most complete foods. A multi-vitamin. *(Best taken on an empty stomach before other food).*
	• Glow promoting food.
	• Helps to carry oxygen around the body, which is important for radiance.
	• High in chlorophyll – cleans the digestive tract *(helping to prevent constipation – remember if you suffer with constipation this can cause inflammation).*
	• Contains more chlorophyll than any other plant. Chlorophyll rejuvenates the blood and cleans the bowels.
	• Extremely alkalizing to the body, helping to balance your PH.
	• Around 60% protein, but contains all essential amino acids to form a complete protein.
	• Contains beta-carotene (vitamin A), B vitamins,

	vitamin E, vitamin C, calcium, zinc, iron, which all contribute to healthy skin and blood flow to promote better circulation and a glowing skin.
	• A rich source of magnesium, which is important for energy production and muscle strength.
	• Potent detoxifying properties. Helps to eliminate heavy metals and other toxins from the body. Great for autoimmune diseases.
	• Greatly decreases the bumpy look of cellulite.
	• Helps fight candida like spirulina.
	• Good source of friendly bacteria. Causes the lactobacilli bacteria in our stomachs to multiply. Taken with meals, helps to improve digestion and assimilation of nutrients.
	• Has been associated with weight loss due to its high levels of nutrients.
	• Boosts immune system.
	• Helps digestion (heals intestinal lining) GREAT FOR LEAKY GUT and other gut problems.
	• Slows aging!

	• Capable of removing alcohol from the liver. *Known to help with hangovers.* • Helps to absorb toxins from the intestines. Toxins in the intestines cause dis-ease and BAD SKIN plus premature aging.
Sprouts *(Broccoli, sunflower, fenugreek, alfalfa, clover etc.).*	• A good supply of plant protein. • Powerful foods for cellular rejuvenation, health and beautiful skin, hair and nails. • Cleanse your body; nourish your cells and tissues. • Give you a beautiful glow from the inside out. • Easy for you to digest. • Full of antioxidants, protein, enzymes and minerals.
Strawberries – A BEAUTY FRUIT.	• Enhance your natural true beauty. • High in vitamin C, this helps to keep the skin's elasticity and also regenerates new cells. • They keep skin youthful, keeping wrinkles at bay. • Also rich in omega-3 fatty acids (in the seeds). Anti-inflammatory. • Good source of magnesium and copper,

	which are all essential for beautiful hair and skin.
Sunflower Seeds – GLOW SEEDS.	• Known to give you a magnetic inner glow as they help you achieve glowing skin from the inside out. • High in vitamin E – rids the body of free radicals that cause cellular damage (anti-aging). • Anti-inflammatory properties. • Contain selenium and magnesium, a lack of which can cause constipation and an unhealthy gut. • Good for fibre, vitamins B1, B5, and folate. • Filled with healthy beauty fats. • High in amino acids, helping to build protein. • Known as happy seeds as they contain tryptophan, which aids in the production of serotonin. Serotonin is made in the gut.
Sweet Potatoes	• High in beta-carotene, which converts to skin brightening vitamin A in the body. Vitamin A is needed to heal the gut. • Protect against sun damage, cancer, heart disease, inflammation, asthma and arthritis.

	<ul><li>Rich in biotin (vitamin B7 – healthy hair), B2, B6, C and E.</li><li>Iron, potassium, copper, manganese and folate.</li><li>Low in sugar.</li><li>High in fibre, maintain stable blood sugar levels.</li></ul>
Turmeric – A Powerful Superfood.	<ul><li>Outstanding health and beauty properties.</li><li>Anti-inflammatory.</li><li>Cleanses the blood.</li><li>Increases circulation and aids in tissue healing.</li><li>Makes skin more glowing, supple and healthy looking.</li><li>Anti-aging.</li><li>Reduces water retention, making the body look slimmer and toned.</li><li>Heals arthritic conditions.</li><li>Fights depression and anxiety.</li></ul>
Walnuts	<ul><li>High in omega-3 fatty acids. Great for brain health. Keeps Alzheimer's away.</li><li>Promote beautiful, glowing skin and hair.</li><li>Give skin a younger looker, smoother appearance.</li><li>Rich in vitamin E.</li><li>High in protein, fibre, some B vitamins, magnesium, calcium,</li></ul>

	potassium, manganese and copper. • Contain L-arginine (an amino acid that helps with healing and repair of collagen). • Naturally contain melatonin to ensure a good night's sleep.
Watercress – Another Beauty Food.	• Cleanse and oxygenate tissues. • Helps heal anaemia. • Full of calcium, iodine, sulphur, manganese and copper. • High in vitamins A, C and E. • Useful at treating acne and eczema. • Highly alkaline. • Invigorates circulation and enhances healthy blood flow to help cleanse toxins from the body, this brings colour to the skin, face, lips and eyes. Great anti-aging/glow food. • Known to also be a cellulite killing food.
Wheatgrass *(acts in our bodies like a detergent, purging the liver, scrubbing the intestinal tract and oxygenating the blood).*	• An effective healer because it contains ALL minerals. • Extremely rich in protein. Contains 17 amino acids. • Wheatgrass juice contains up to 70% chlorophyll – an

	important blood builder. Great for beautiful skin.
	• High in vitamins A, B-complex, C, E and K.
	• Full of beautifying enzymes.
	• Improves digestion.
	• Increases energy.
	• Cleans liver.
	• Detoxifies the body.
	• Helps with weight loss.
	• Slows down aging.
	• Anti-inflammatory.
	• Clears skin.

Chapter 40
Health and Beauty Minerals

"Around 95% of the body's activities are run by minerals, NOT vitamins. Our bio-chemistry is mineral dependent." – David Avocado Wolfe

The beauty and health of our skin, hair, nails, etc. all depend on how mineralised we are. Minerals are required for rejuvenation, beauty and true health.

Minerals are NECESSARY to build our beauty and health.

Here Is A List Of A Few Of Them And Their Benefits:

Silicon	<ul><li>An incredible insulator. Keeps the blood warm.</li><li>Silicon is transformed into calcium.</li><li>Has been shown to increase bone-mineral density.</li><li>May reverse the formation of cavities.</li><li>Silicon is a yoga mineral – meaning it allows for flexibility and elasticity.</li><li>The highest concentration is found in the hair and nails. It makes our hair thick and our nails strong.</li><li>One is considered to be more youthful when there is more silicon</li></ul>

	in your body. Can improve wrinkles. • Found in foods and herbs such as, horsetail, nettles, hemp leaf/seeds, romaine lettuce, burdock root, bell peppers (in the fruits skin), oats (steel-cut oatmeal), cucumbers (in the skin), alfalfa, brown rice, apples, almonds, flaxseeds, radishes, green superfood powders and tomatoes (in the skin).
Sulphur	• The mineral for ALL beauty. • Makes the complexion glow and gives you beautiful hair. **The best beauty cosmetic.** • Helps relieve any pain or inflammation. • Repairs tissues. • It gives connective tissues its strength, ensuring strong bones, ligaments and tendons. • Eliminates any muscle cramps. • A vital mineral for detoxification. • Found in foods such as rocket, blue-green algae, bee pollen, durian, broccoli, garlic, Brussels sprouts, hemp seeds, kale, maca powder, onions, noni juice, pumpkin seeds, spirulina, watercress and cabbage.
Zinc – also TOP list for beauty.	• Is involved in digestion and metabolism. Needed for a healthy gut. • Is essential for beautiful skin and is also required for, cell and bodily growth, sexual development, fertility, night vison and balancing blood sugar.

	• When taken with vitamin A and sulphur, it builds strong, lustrous hair.
	• Prevents wrinkled skin, stretch marks, radiation damage and is helpful for acne as well as other skin conditions and signs of aging. It is needed to stimulate collagen production.
	• Very important for the health of the reproductive system.
	• Best sources of zinc are pumpkin seeds, watermelon seeds, garlic, cashew nuts, pine nuts, macadamia nuts, sunflower seeds, sesame seeds, coconuts, spirulina and seaweeds.
Iron	• 2/3rds of iron is found in the blood. Iron-rich haemoglobin in the blood carries oxygen throughout the body.
	• An iron deficiency creates a low level of oxygenation in the blood, resulting in weakness, light-headedness, fatigue etc.
	• Healthy, oxygenated blood stimulates good circulation, resulting in beautiful, glowing skin.
	• Low iron may result in limp hair and possibly hair loss.
	• If you have a leaky gut, this is also known to cause an iron deficiency – heal and seal your gut.
	• Look for iron in, onions, cacao (raw chocolate), cherries, nettles, parsley, spinach, kale, (most dark leafy greens), most red-coloured berries, spirulina, chlorella, beetroots and chia seeds.

Magnesium – Another Beauty Mineral!	• A key mineral for keeping our bowels regular *(if you are constipated regularly you may need more magnesium in your diet).*
	• Helps you to remain fit, young and energetic.
	• A lack of magnesium makes your body feel weak and may age you more rapidly.
	• It helps the body maintain normal nerve and muscle function.
	• Keeps your bones strong. Prevents osteoporosis as it helps your body absorb calcium.
	• Boosts your immunity.
	• Relieves muscle soreness and is known to cure headaches.
	• Is very effective in reducing wrinkles and fine lines.
	• Helps to combat breakouts or acne.
	• A deficiency in magnesium leads to hair loss and scalp bolding.
	• Promotes sleep.
	• It detoxifies and cleanses the skin.
	• Good for the lymphatic system.
	• Foods high in magnesium are: dark leafy greens, nuts and seeds, avocados, bananas, raw dark chocolate (cacao) and oatmeal.
Potassium *(Is so important to every living thing that without it there would be no life).*	• Is an electrolyte.
	• You must have potassium to build and maintain youthful, healthy tissues.
	• Is needed for cellular cleansing.
	• Helps muscles to keep their control over the body.
	• Helps with the growth of new cells.

	- Helps to relieve any stressful situations you might have. Reducing anxiety. - A deficiency causes fatigue, irritability, high blood pressure. - May be called the detergent of the arteries. - Potassium rich foods are; avocados, dark leafy greens, raw apple cider vinegar, celery, coconuts, bananas, nuts and seeds, dried figs and dates.
Calcium	- Keeps our bones strong. Helps us to move gracefully. - Wards of PMS. - Good for the heart. - A strengthening mineral. - Found in foods such as; ALL dark leafy greens like kale, Swiss chard, spinach, Bok choy, beet tops and broccoli. Also in figs, oranges and almonds. Moringa powder/ leaf is a superfood packed with calcium. DO NOT EAT DAIRY! It is highly acidic to the body, making you leach calcium from your bones causing osteoporosis. - Also AVOID Calcium supplements as they may cause you to rapidly age.
Selenium	- Antioxidant and anti-inflammatory. - Needed to heal a leaky gut. - Anti-aging. Boosts collagen in the skin. - Found in foods such as; Brazil nuts, brown or black rice, dark leafy greens, chia seeds, sesame seeds and sunflower seeds.

Avoid inorganic minerals such as chlorine, fluoride, calcium carbonate, aluminium, lead etc. These clog the arteries and small capillaries that are needed to feed and nourish your brain with oxygenated blood; the result is gradual loss of memory, senility and strokes. Fluoride is also linked to autoimmune diseases and thyroid problems.

Chapter 41
Spices and Herbs for Health and Beauty

Healthy Spices/Herbs	Beauty and Health Benefits
Turmeric	<ul><li>Anti-inflammatory, works well as prescription anti-inflammatories.</li><li>Antioxidant.</li><li>High in curcumin, a natural painkiller.</li><li>Helps clean the blood.</li><li>Helps tissues to rejuvenate.</li><li>Increases energy.</li><li>Fights pimples/acne.</li><li>Adds colour to the skin.</li><li>Prevents hardening of the arteries.</li><li>Supports collagen. Anti-aging.</li><li>Strengthens immune system.</li><li>Heals the gut.</li><li>Known to fight depression.</li><li>Heals painful joints.</li></ul>
Cumin	<ul><li>Natural pain killer.</li><li>Good source of iron.</li><li>Vitamins C and E.</li><li>Combats insomnia.</li><li>Helps with digestion.</li></ul>

	• Helpful at treating skin disorders and reduces signs of premature aging.
Coriander	• Aids digestion. • Lowers blood sugar levels. • Natural antibiotic. • Good for cholesterol. • Pulls heavy metals from the body. • Anti-inflammatory. • Skin boosting vitamin C – anti-aging.
Cayenne Pepper	• Used for detox. • Stimulates circulation / supports lymphatic system. • Aids digestion – heals upset stomachs. • Boosts metabolism, helpful for burning fat. • Anti-inflammatory. Good for intestinal permeability (leaky gut).
Ginger	• Reduces workout soreness. • Anti-inflammatory. • Natural antibiotic. • Boosts attention, focus and memory. • Helpful for acne sufferers. • Boosts immune system.
Nutmeg	• Anti-inflammatory and anti-bacterial. • Fights acne. • Stimulates hair growth.
Cloves	• Helps rid digestive tract of unwanted bacteria and parasites. • Also great for oral health. • Contain omega-3 fatty acids, which are anti-inflammatory.

	•	Improve digestion.
Black pepper	•	Contains piperine, which helps the body burn more fat.
	•	Helps body use nutrients more effectively.
	•	Treats minor digestive problems.
	•	Rich source of magnesium, potassium and vitamins C and K. Good for fine lines and wrinkles.
	•	Helps the body absorb nutrients from food.
Cinnamon	•	Aids digestion.
	•	Balances blood sugar levels (stops cravings).
	•	Antioxidant.
	•	Improves circulation.
	•	Gut healing.
	•	Anti-inflammatory.
	•	Fights acne.
	•	Slows the signs of aging.
Mustard seeds	•	Boost metabolic rate.
	•	Slow down aging and help your skin to look radiant.
	•	Rich source of vitamin A – great for hair health.
	•	Contain selenium and magnesium.
Curry leaf	•	Aids digestion.
	•	Aids weight loss.
	•	Protects liver.
	•	Good for digestion.
	•	Cancer-fighting properties.
Oregano	•	Anti-inflammatory.
	•	Anti-fungal.
	•	Improves bone density.
	•	Good for skin.
	•	Antioxidant.
	•	Helpful for candida.

	• Anti-aging.
	• Treats acid reflux.
Rosemary	• Boosts memory, concentration and focus.
	• Relieves stress.
	• Antioxidant.
	• Anti-microbial and anti-inflammatory.
	• Boosts immune system.
	• Great for skin and hair health. Helpful for hair loss.
	• Anti-aging.
Thyme	• Strong anti-bacterial.
	• Anti-microbial.
	• Reduces blood pressure.
	• Keeps premature aging at bay.
	• Makes skin soft, supple and radiant.
	• Increases collagen production.
	• Aids in the treatment of acne.
	• Promotes hair growth as high in the mineral zinc.
Garlic Powder or granules	• Natural sodium.
	• Strengthens immune system.
	• Contains the beauty mineral sulphur.

This is just a selection of herbs and spices. There are many more to choose from. Be creative, they all have wonderful beauty and health benefits, plus they make your food taste good too.

Chapter 42

Summary

Heal Your Gut for Beauty and Longevity

Remove Toxins From Your Diet Such As:

1. **Gluten** – this causes a HUGE amount of inflammation in the gut and is known to be one of the biggest causes of leaky gut syndrome. When the holes in your gut are inflamed and open this may then develop into future health problems such as, autoimmune disorders like Graves' disease, Rheumatoid arthritis, Celiac disease, Psoriasis and even thyroid issues. Gluten is one of the biggest causes of autoimmunity today. It is estimated currently that there are over 100 autoimmune diseases and this is growing rapidly. Most of us have one now and don't know it yet. All autoimmune diseases are caused by inflammation. You HAVE to remove gluten! However, it's not easy because gluten is in EVERYTHING from toothpastes, to lipsticks, it's even in shampoo – it is everywhere. In Latin gluten means glue and that is what it does when you eat it – it sticks to your insides and causes dis-ease. We lack the enzymes to break down and absorb gluten and also our immune system / gut see gluten as an invader. Every time you eat gluten the protein zonulin is released. This opens the tiny holes in your small intestinal net into larger holes. This then causes undigested food particles to slip into the bloodstream. As a result chronic inflammation begins in the body, which may then lead to future health problems and maybe even skin issues. We do not want to let this happen. Avoid gluten as much

as you can. It is also NOT a beauty food. If it is causing your gut inflammation, it will also be a cause of skin inflammation. What goes on inside the gut usually reflects on the outside too.

Be More Careful With Your Food Choices.

Instead of having bread change it for:

- Quinoa bread.
- Brown rice cakes with no added salt.
- Raw dehydrated crackers.
- Oat cakes.
- Buckwheat bread etc.

There are so many different options out there today, which makes it a lot easier BUT avoid the gluten-free aisles. Most gluten-free products HAVE had the gluten removed however; in its place toxic chemicals and emulsifiers etc. have been added for extra taste and texture that cause cancer and more.

2. **Remove Sugar** – sugar is a poison and very toxic to your body. It leads to strokes and heart attacks as well as leaky gut and it ages you fast. If you want to age fast, keep taking in sugar. It causes CHRONIC inflammation in the body and is another big factor in all dis-ease and skin problems. Sugar is not a food, it is DEADLY! Sugar also causes hormonal issues. If you know you have a hormonal imbalance, I would suggest you look to see how much sugar you are taking in on a daily basis and don't be fooled by artificial sweeteners, these wreak havoc on your hormones.

3. **Remove Dairy** – dairy goes through a pasteurization process that destroys enzymes and probiotics. Cow's milk also contains a protein known as casein and is known to cause inflammation in the body the same as gluten. Dairy is also a cause of PCOS, acne, oestrogen dominance and other hormonal issues as well as autoimmune diseases.

If you wish to have milk, use goats or sheep instead. These are easier for our bodies to digest or simply change to unsweetened almond milks, coconut milk etc. just be careful they aren't loaded with extra sugars and preservatives. Better to make your own.

Add Supplements To Your Diet Such As:

1. **Probiotics** – restoring beneficial bacteria to the gut is ESSENTIAL. This may be accomplished by taking a probiotic supplement that contains good bacteria such as Bifidobacterium and Lactobacillus species. I recommend anywhere from 10 billion forming units to 100 billion units a day. They also need to contain 10 or more strains and are preferably soil based. Probiotics are known to switch off any inflammation in the body. Eating fermented foods daily is also HIGHLY recommended. Consuming foods high in fibre is also very important. These are prebiotics, which help to grow your good army of probiotics. Fibre is needed daily from plant based foods such as dark-leafy greens.

2. **Digestive Enzymes** – protease, amylase, lipase, glucoamylase, alpha-galactosidase. You can buy in supplement form if needed and take before a meal. These help you to break down foods easier. Recommended if you do have a leaky gut.

3. **Omega-3 Fatty Acids** – these decrease inflammation in the body and when you mix with exercise they are also helpful for burning unwanted fat. DO NOT BE SCARED OF HEALTHY FAT! They will not make you fat. These are the building blocks for beautiful, glowing and radiant skin. Ladies listen up, you have to eat healthy fat for good skin, hair and balanced hormones. Fat is one of the MOST IMPORTANT elements in good skin health.

    Research also suggests that if you take fish oils daily your chances for getting a headache are decreased. Reason for this is because they are anti-inflammatory. We need omega-3 fats for brain and gut health as well as lubrication for our joints, radiant skin and healthy hair follicles. Look for fish oils with DHA and EPA. 4-6 grams is needed to heal your gut and 1-2 grams for your everyday average person. DHA is a building block of tissue in the brain and retina of the eye; it also helps with brain function. It is great for pregnant women as it helps with the foetus brain development. As we get older our levels of EPA and DHA decline. Research is now suggesting that Alzheimer's and dementia may be caused by a lack of EPA (eicosapentaenoic acid) and DHA (docosahexaenoic acid) in our bodies. EPA has also been shown to help with childhood behaviour, academic performance and focus, plus inflammatory conditions such as eczema and acne. Research also states that mental health issues, including depression and dyslexia may be down to low levels of EPA in adults'. This once again is caused by inflammation. Omega fats are also needed for joint and bone problems as well as heart issues, energy, dry, flaking skin and to cushion tissues and organs.

To achieve strong, healthy hair and smooth glowing skin this requires a daily intake of essential fatty acids (EFAs). They help to keep the skin nourished and supple from within. Our bodies crave fats because cells use our good fats to regenerate and build new tissue. When looking at what fats to eat daily these are the best kind, walnuts, chia, flaxseeds, hemp seeds, pumpkin seeds, sunflower seeds and the best fat of all – AVOCADO! Fats are a MUST in your diet to heal your gut, to regulate your hormones, and to control excess sebum production in acne prone skin. DO NOT SKIP THE HEALTHY FATS!

4. Take gut wall healers such as L-Glutamine – an amino acid that helps to rejuvenate the gut lining, sealing the holes in your net. L-Glutamine can be found naturally in beans, goji berries, spinach, parsley and red cabbage but our bodies need such a huge amount if we are trying to heal the gut, therefore it is advised to take in powder form, twice a day before food. Other key nutrients to heal the gut are **zinc carnosine, vitamins A, C, E and**

D as well as herbs such as slippery elm, MSM sulphur, liquorice root and aloe vera.

5. Support your liver function with milk thistle, l-glutamine and cleansing liver juices such as celery. I really recommend you start juicing daily – not blending. Juicing will help to heal the gut, more so than blending and as a side effect you will also have glowing skin.

- **Eat organic where you can.** Avoid the pesticide sprays they also destroy your gut.
- **Drink lots of water.** The best thing to clean your colon is to start your day with 500ml – 1 litre of water when you wake up. Our bodies need to be hydrated to prevent bad bacteria propelling through our digestive track. Drinking water also keeps your skin youthful and hydrated. Water helps keep you looking younger as it reduces wrinkles by filling in and plumping out the skin. Try your best to not drink water during meals. It dilutes your beauty enzymes and slows down digestion. Remember this; *you do not need liquid with your meals.* You may have water 20 minutes before meals or at least 30-60 minutes after you have eaten. To prepare your gut for digestion you could also drink raw unfiltered 'With Mother' apple cider vinegar 20 minutes prior to eating.
- **Give your digestive system a rest.** Our gut cannot rest and repair when we over eat. Try and fast or cleanse once a week or once a month. 15–17 hours is a good starting point (this is known as intermittent fasting). Fasting has also been proven to heal the gut. **There is not a food or supplement that heals you – your body heals itself.**
- **Eat plenty of fermentable fibres** like sweet potatoes, dark leafy greens etc., and any plant based foods. These are known as prebiotics.
- **Eat fermented foods** like kefir and sauerkraut daily.
- **Take coconut products** – these are high in Lauric acid, which kills pathogens such as bacteria and fungi. ALL coconut products are great for gut health.

- **Drink green juice** – heals EVERYTHING!
- **Take Aloe Vera** – also helps to keep the colon clean and get things moving. Take every day. A daily dose of aloe vera helps to calm down the belly. Good for inflammation.
- Make **green smoothies** every day!! Half the drink should be dark leafy greens and the rest some kind of fruit or water. We need fibre daily. Remember fibre is a prebiotic that helps to feed the probiotics in your gut, which enable you to populate and grow your good bacteria for beautiful skin and good health. The fastest, strongest, leanest and most muscular animals eat primarily greens. Greens provide us with amino acids we need to build muscle but they are also the most powerful way to get those beauty minerals into our body. Green plants are our number one food source for providing us with all the minerals that we need for *beauty* and *good health*. Greens are also the best thing to keep our digestive system in tip top condition. A good gut keeps us healthy for life. My favourite way to get more greens into the body is by juicing and blending. **EAT GREEN!** *(Greens make you lean and strong plus they are* ANTI-INFLAMMATORY*)*.
- **Take turmeric** – research shows it heals ALL inflammation and has been shown to reverse depression and arthritis. Always take with a healthy fat such as coconut oil and black pepper.
- **Take ginger** – a natural antibiotic and anti-inflammatory food.
- **Eat olives and olive oil** – very powerful antioxidants with anti-inflammatory effects. Also known to beautify the skin. When purchasing buy in a glass, dark bottle and make sure it is cold-pressed. There are a lot of toxic brands on the market today, be careful. Do not buy out of a plastic bottle.
- **Take oregano oil** – gets rid of the bad bacteria. Helpful for killing off parasites in the body. Also anti-inflammatory.

- Take steps to **manage stress**. Chronic stress causes severe inflammation, which is bad news for our health and skin. – Why not take up yoga? Or do something that makes you feel happy.
- Eat foods rich in **polyphenols** such as dark chocolate, cherries, apples, blackberries and drink green tea.

> **Inflammation is the body's way of saying something is wrong.**

- Eat more **anti-inflammatory foods** such as:

Almonds	Avocado	Eat beta-carotene rich foods such as sweet potatoes, carrots, watermelon etc.
Cinnamon	Garlic	Vitamin C rich fruits – oranges, kiwi, goji berries, baobab etc.
Strawberries	Green Tea / Matcha. Has been shown to heal leaky gut.	Cruciferous vegetables – broccoli, cauliflower, cabbage etc.
Spinach, Kale, Swiss Chard etc. – ALL dark, leafy greens.	Olives / Olive Oil.	Omega-3 foods: Walnuts, pecans. flaxseeds, wild-caught salmon, chia seeds, spirulina, kiwi fruits etc.
Spirulina and Chlorella.	Red onions / red apples (Quercetin).	Dark coloured fruits – all berries, red grapes etc.

> **Raw dark chocolate (cacao) – no sugar (70-100%).**

A diet high in meat, sugar, gluten, hydrogenated oils, processed foods, sodas, artificial food additives and dairy all encourage inflammation. A diet high in omega-3 fats, found in flax, chia seeds, oily fish as well as green algae's from the sea switch off inflammation.

Too much inflammation in the body is when we develop conditions such as autoimmune diseases, cancer, skin problems, premature aging and more. Inflammation causes damage to your cells. This not only destroys your body internally but also leads to puffy eyes, saggy skin, wrinkles, bloating, acne, psoriasis, hair loss and more. We have to combat inflammation if we wish to heal. The first step is to change how we eat. You have to eliminate inflammatory foods from your diet and replace with anti-inflammatory foods.

- **Try to eat more raw foods.** You do not need to become a raw foodist or fully vegan. Just make a conscious effort to add more raw plant-based foods to your diet every day.

> **A good goal would be to add one piece of raw food with every meal or snack. Preferably eat it before your meal and make sure it's green, for example a cucumber, celery stick or green salad. ANYTHING GREEN!**

We mentioned earlier about the importance of enzymes. Raw foods are rich in enzymes (fresh fruits and vegetables). These enzymes are your *'fountain of youth'*, which we want to keep topped up as much as we can. When we eat more raw food it adds extra enzymes to our beauty and health bank account. This is what we want. Eat in abundance daily.

Food is the fuel on which every cell in our bodies runs, so eating dead, lifeless food can only lead to compromised health and beauty.

- **Eat your suntan**. Certain foods will give you a healthy glow from the inside out. Carotenoids give the skin a beautiful sun kissed, attractive glow. Add more carotenoid rich foods to your daily meals such as; carrots, sweet potatoes, spinach, collard, greens, squash, bell peppers, coriander, pink grapefruit, tomatoes, watermelon, pumpkin etc.

- **Eat more 'Sprouts'** – see chapter on sprouts for their amazing health and beauty benefits. They also help to heal the gut.

- ***Try not to eat food after 8 pm and be in bed by 10 pm***. Digestion takes up A LOT of energy. Ideally, we need a 3 hour gap after eating before we go to bed to enable food to digest before sleep. If you go to bed on a belly full of food, your body will only be working on digestion and not cleaning and repairing. This means you will be unable to rejuvenate properly at night. Ideally, you should sleep between 10 pm and wake up by 6 am, feeling refreshed. 8 hours of sleep is the recommended amount. If you also do not get enough sleep, your gut health suffers as do your hormones.

- **Vitamin D** (The Sun) – there is a huge epidemic today of vitamin D deficiency. Vitamin D is also needed for a healthy, beautiful body and without it; it can lead to cancers, autoimmune disorders, osteoporosis, hormonal problems, gut problems, depression and so much more. Try to get at least 10 minutes of sun exposure per day WITHOUT sun screen to get your daily dose or eat more vitamin D rich foods such as; egg yolks, mushrooms and oily fish. Vitamin D turns on more healing genes than any substance yet known.

- **Vitamin A** – is important for your body to grow and repair itself and helps support a healthy immune system. It is also needed to help your intestines absorb zinc. Found in cashews, chickpeas etc.

- **Exercise** has been shown to provide a positive boost to beneficial strains in the gut and may shut down inflammation, especially yoga.

> The digestive tract is one of the most regenerative parts of the body and, with the best diet; the majority of digestive problems can be resolved. – Patrick Holford.

Studies show that gut flora can begin to change within 3 days but you have to be consistent.

If you are dealing with an autoimmune disease, it may take 6 months – one year to fully heal. Be kind to yourself and be patient. This didn't happen overnight, it will take time.

I hope you can see now that having a healthy gut is central to your entire health and beauty and is connected to EVERYTHING in your body.

BEAUTY AND HEALTH BEGINS IN THE GUT.

Don't forget to go to my Instagram @holistic_dani for new updates or join me on my Facebook page: www.facebook.com/holisticlivingforlife

Chapter 43
Beauty and the Gut Recipes

Juices

Anti-Aging Beauty – Carrot and Cucumber Juice

Ingredients:
- Carrots x 2
- Cucumber x 3 (small)
- Celery x 2
- Green apple x 1 (preferably organic)
- Lemon x 1
- Fresh coconut water (optional).

Directions:
- Always put one apple in first and then juice the other ingredients.
- Optional – mix fresh coconut water to the juice.

Beauty Facts:
- Cucumbers for glowing skin.
- Lemons fight wrinkles.
- Carrots create gorgeous hair.
- Apples cleanse the body.
- Celery reduces stress hormones.

Cucumber and Kale

Ingredients:

- Kale x 3 dinosaur
- Cucumber x 5 baby
- Green apple x 1 (preferably organic)
- Handful of mint leaves
- ½ a lemon
- Fresh coconut water (optional).

Directions:

- Always put one apple in first and then juice the other ingredients.
- Optional – mix coconut water to the juice.

Beauty Facts:

- Cucumbers for glowing skin.
- Kale high in iron.
- Mint promotes digestion.
- Apples cleanse the body.

Glorious Glowing Green Goddess

Ingredients:

- 3 big handfuls of spinach
- Large bunch kale
- 1-3 pieces of broccoli with stem
- 3 small cucumbers
- 1 organic green apple or 2
- 1-2 celery stalks
- ½ a lemon
- 1 inch of ginger.
- 1 coconut water (optional).

Directions:

- Place all ingredients into the juicer. Optional – mix fresh coconut water to the juice.

The Disease Fighter

Ingredients:

- 1 handful of mint
- 1 handful of parsley
- 1 lemon
- 1 green apple
- Ginger ½ inch
- Turmeric root ½ inch
- Celery x 2
- Cucumber x 2
- ½ a red pepper
- Dandelion greens.

Beauty Benefits:

- Reduces inflammation.
- It soothes the nervous system. The minerals magnesium will also calm you down if you are feeling stressed.
- It contains 'good' salts, which are natural and essential for your health.

Directions:

- Always put one apple in first and then juice the other ingredients.
- Optional – mix coconut water to the juice.

Beauty Benefits:

Parsley – purifies blood and is great for cellulite.

Ginger and turmeric – both fight inflammation and give you good circulation, which means a healthy glow.

Dandelion Greens – cleans liver, great for skin and hair health.

Smoothies

The Anti-Inflammatory
Ingredients:

- 1 tbsp. soaked chia seeds
- ½ tsp fresh grated ginger
- ½ tsp turmeric
- 1 scoop protein powder (vegan)
- ½ frozen banana
- 1 cup frozen pineapple
- Fresh coconut water.

Directions:

Blend and serve.

The Beauty Elixir
Ingredients:

- Fresh coconut water
- ½ cup coconut milk (full fat, organic)
- 1 tbsp. acai
- 1 tbsp. goji berries
- 1 tbsp. spirulina or chlorella
- 1 tbsp. raw cacao
- 1 tbsp. maca
- 1 tbsp. bee pollen
- 1 tbsp. soaked chia seeds
- 1 tbsp. vegan rice protein powder
- 1 tbsp. moringa powder.
- Optional add ½ cup of blueberries.

Directions:
- Blend. This will have you glowing and full of energy.

Creamy Blueberries
Ingredients:
- Blueberries ½ cup
- 1/2 an avocado
- Big handful of spinach
- Coconut milk or water
- 1 tbsp. goji berries.

Directions:
- Blend.

Cucumber and Avocado
Ingredients:
- 3 organic cucumbers (baby)
- ½ avocado
- Coconut water.

Directions:
- Blend all ingredients together.

Breakfasts

Skin Glowing Smoothie Bowl
Ingredients:
- 1 frozen banana
- Acai berry (frozen or in powder form)
- 50g frozen berries
- 250 ml nut milk, coconut water or coconut milk
- 1 tsp vanilla extract

- 1 tbsp. chia seeds, pumpkin seeds, cacao nibs, goji berries and desiccated coconut for topping.

Directions:

- Blend banana, berries, acai, vanilla extract and coconut water or milk.
- Place in a bowl and top with seeds and coconut etc.

Sexy Abs
Ingredients:

- 1 handful of kale
- 1 handful of coriander
- 8 celery stalks
- ½ a lemon
- 1 inch ginger
- 2 cucumbers (baby)
- 1 green apple.

Directions:
- Send through a juicer.

Beauty Juice

The key ingredient for beauty here is the beetroot.

Ingredients:

- 1-2 small beetroots
- 5-6 celery stalks
- 3 small cucumbers
- ½ lemon
- Big handful of rocket
- 1-2 inch of ginger
- 1 green apple (always try to get organic).

Directions:

- Place through juicer.

Chia Porridge
Ingredients:

- 3-5 tbsp. chia seeds
- 1 heaped tbsp. of cacao powder
- 1 heaped tbsp. maca powder
- 1 tbsp. bee pollen
- 1 tbsp. hemp seeds
- 1 tbsp. cinnamon.

Directions:

- Soak chia seeds in water the night before. You may also soak in morning but leave for 15-20 minutes before eating. Stir until they turn into a gel consistency.
- Add cacao powder; pour over a little hot water from the kettle to let the cacao melt into chia seeds.
- Stir in the other superfoods.
- Serve with extra toppings, e.g. berries, pumpkin seeds, coconut flakes, cacao nibs, cinnamon, fruit etc. Whatever you fancy.

Banana Chocolate Strawberry and Chia Pudding
Ingredients:

- 1 banana
- ½ cup strawberries
- 1 tbsp. cacao powder
- 1 tbsp. maca powder
- 1 tbsp. bee pollen
- 100 ml coconut milk
- 2 – 4 tbsp. chia seeds.

Directions:

- Add the banana, cacao, maca, bee pollen, strawberries and coconut milk into a blender.

- Stir mixture into chia seeds. Give a good stir so chia seeds look like gel.
- Leave to set for 10-20 minutes or soak overnight.
- Top with fresh fruits or any superfoods you wish.

Lunches

Kale Salad with Lemon Dressing
Ingredients:
- 4 cups of chopped kale
- 1 avocado, diced
- ½ cup cooked quinoa
- ¼ cup pomegranate seeds
- ½ cup chopped pecans
- ¼ cup olive oil
- ¼ cup apple cider vinegar
- ½ lemon squeezed
- Zest of 1 lemon.

Directions:
- To make the dressing, whisk together olive oil, apple cider, lemon juice and zest.
- Place kale in a large bowl, top with avocado, pomegranate, and pecans.
- Prepare the dressing. Pour on top. Stir and serve.

Tabbouleh Salad with Pine Nuts
Ingredients:
- 1 huge bunch of parsley
- ½ white onion, diced
- 1 tomato, diced
- 1 tbsp. pine nuts
- Juice of 1 lemon
- 1 garlic clove, minced
- ¼ cup cold-pressed olive oil
- Black pepper.

Directions:

- Chop the parsley and place in a large bowl, along with the onion, tomato and pine nuts.
- In a blender, combine the lemon, garlic and black pepper. Blend.
- Pour the dressing over the salad and mix well. Enjoy!

Broccoli Soup
Ingredients:

- 1 broccoli
- 1 400ml can of coconut milk (organic / full fat)
- Black pepper
- Nutmeg.

Directions:

- Add the coconut milk and broccoli to a pan and bring to boil. Let simmer for around 5 minutes until the broccoli softens. Remove from heat.
- After letting it cool, transfer to a blender and process until smooth.
- Transfer back to pan and add black pepper and nutmeg.
- Serve with optional toppings such as avocado or macadamia nuts.

Sweet Potato and Quinoa Soup
Ingredients:

- 1 cup quinoa
- 2 large sweet potatoes
- 1 small onion
- 1 can of black beans (organic – no added salt)
- 1 can of diced tomatoes (organic – no added salt)
- 1 tsp. minced garlic
- 1 tsp. chili powder
- 5 cups of organic vegetable broth – optional
- Parsley
- Black pepper.

Directions:
- Add 1 tbsp. coconut oil to the pan. Add sweet potato, onion, garlic and stir together.
- Add quinoa, and broth. Bring to boil and then simmer until quinoa is cooked. Around 15-20 minutes.
- Add in tomatoes, beans and seasoning.
- Serve.

Main Meals

Basil Pesto Pasta
Ingredients:
- Heaps of fresh basil
- 3 garlic cloves
- 1/2 cup pumpkin seeds
- 5 tbsp. nutritional yeast flakes
- 4–5 tbsp. olive oil
- Optional a handful of kale or parsley
- ½ fresh lemon juice squeezed
- Water depending on how thick you want the sauce
- Black pepper.

Directions:
- Place all of the ingredients into a blender and blend.
- Prepare gluten-free pasta or spaghetti. Follow directions on packet.
- Pour pesto over the pasta.
- Serve with a large green salad or steamed vegetables with a splash of apple cider vinegar.
- Enjoy.

Sweet Potato and Red Lentil Stew
Ingredients:
- 1 onion, diced
- 4 garlic cloves

- 2 sweet potatoes
- 3 cups of organic vegetable broth
- ½ cup red lentils
- 1 can diced tomatoes (organic – no added salt or sugar)
- 3 tbsp. tomato paste (organic)
- 1 can organic full fat coconut milk (398ml, 14 ounce)
- 1 ½ tsps. ground turmeric
- 1 ½ teaspoons ground cumin
- ½ teaspoon chili powder
- ¼ teaspoon cayenne pepper
- Black pepper
- 3 tbsp. apple cider vinegar (raw with mother)
- 1 bunch chard or kale.

Directions:
- Add 1 tbsp. coconut oil to pan with onion and garlic. Stir to combine. Sauté for around 3-5 minutes.
- Add the sweet potatoes and stir.
- Add broth, diced tomatoes, coconut milk, lentils, tomato paste, turmeric, cumin, chili, cayenne pepper, black pepper and stir well to combine.
- Simmer for around 30 minutes, until sweet potatoes are softened.
- Add apple cider vinegar to taste.
- Stir in chard or kale.
- Garnish with coriander.
- Serve with brown rice or vegetables.

Vegetable Turmeric Soup
Ingredients:
- 1 onion, diced
- 1 medium carrot, finely chopped
- 2 stalks of celery, chopped
- 1 tbsp. organic turmeric
- 2 teaspoons garlic powder or 4 cloves
- ½ tsp. ground ginger

- ¼ tsp. ground cayenne
- 3–4 cups of water
- Vegetable broth
- Black pepper
- 3 cups cauliflower florets, chopped
- 1 bunch of kale
- 1 can black beans (organic).

Directions:

- In a large pan add 1 tbsp. coconut oil. Add onion and stir until the onion begins to brown.
- Add carrots and celery, cook for 3–4 minutes, until the vegetables soften.
- Add turmeric, garlic, ginger, and cayenne. Stir until the vegetables are coated. Cook for 1 minute.
- Add broth, water, pepper, and stir.
- Bring to boil, reduce heat to low. Add cauliflower and simmer for around 10–15 minutes till soft.
- When the cauliflower is fork tender, add beans, kale and stir.
- Serve hot.

Sauerkraut

Ingredients:

- 1 large head of cabbage
- 2 tbsp. Celtic sea salt.

Directions:

- Cut the head of cabbage in half, and then into quarters. Cut out the core sections and remove any outer leaves, which may have black spots. Cut into small strips.
- Place all chopped pieces into a large bowl.
- Mix in the 2 tbsp. of sea salt and properly mix it with your hands. Pound the cabbage so it releases water.
- Stomp cabbage and salt together for a good 20 minutes before you have enough liquid to submerge the cabbage.

- Pack sauerkraut into a glass fermentation jar with a lid.
- Place in a dark location away from windows for at least 1 week and wait.
- Generally sauerkraut is finished fermenting after 2 weeks.
- After, refrigerate in a sealed jar. This may keep for 3 months.

Creamy Cashew Sauce
Ingredients:
- ½ cup cashew nuts
- 1 tbsp. pumpkin seeds
- 4 tbsp. nutritional yeast
- Black pepper
- ½ a lime or lemon juiced
- 1 tsp. turmeric powder
- 1 tsp. apple cider vinegar
- 1 tsp. garlic powder
- 1 cup of water.

Directions:
- Place all ingredients into the blender and blend.
- Serve over your favourite gluten free pasta or salad.

Salad Idea:
- 1 purple cabbage shredded.
- Sliced green onions.
- 4 plum tomatoes, sliced.
- ½ a red pepper cut.
- 1 cup of diced celery.
- Shredded carrots.

Dessert

Chocolate Heaven
Ingredients:

- 2 ripe avocados
- 3 tbsp. raw honey
- ¼ cup unsweetened raw cacao powder
- ½ tsp. vanilla extract
- Optional add maca and cinnamon powder for an extra beauty / health kick, they taste really good too.

Directions:

- Use a blender or food processor to blend the avocados until smooth.
- Add the rest of the ingredients and blend again until everything is combined.
- Chill for at least 2 hours before serving.

Healthy Snack Ideas

- Fresh vegetables with homemade hummus or guacamole.
- 1 handful of nuts (preferably soaked).
- Apples with natural nut butters (1 tbsp.)
- 1 cup of berries.
- Goji berries with pumpkin seeds, cacao nibs and coconut flakes.
- Homemade granola bars.
- Green salad.
- Frozen grapes.
- Sugar snap peas.
- Fresh fruit and dip.
- Baked kale chips.
- Frozen chocolate covered bananas (homemade chocolate).
- Celery with nut butters.
- Almonds (10).

- Handful of olives.
- Watermelon.
- Cucumbers and dips.
- Green Juice.
- Green smoothie.
- Spirulina and coconut water.
- Natural plant protein shakes.

The main thing is to never let yourself go hungry or feel deprived. There are so many amazing foods out there that will make your skin glow and help you achieve fabulous health for life.

Always remember:-

BEAUTY AND HEALTH BEGIN IN THE GUT
Dani x

Chapter 44
References

There are many documents, books, websites and seminars whose insights have helped me to write this book. The following list of books is by no means complete; it simply reflects some of the best works that have assisted in the creation of *Beauty and The GUT.*

Alejandro Junger (2013), Clean Gut, (Harper Collins).

Charles Jones (2014), The Ultimate Raw Food Guide.

David Wolfe (2009), Eating for Beauty, (North Atlantic Books, Berkeley, California).

David Wolfe (2013), Longevity Now, (North Atlantic Books, Berkeley, California).

David Wolfe (2009), Superfoods, (North Atlantic Books, Berkeley, California).

Dr. Ann Wigmore (1984), The Hippocrates Diet and Health Programme, (New York, Avery).

Dr Joseph Mercola (2002), Soy is an Endocrine Distributor and Can Disrupt Your Child's Health (Mercola.com).

Dr Josh Axe (2016) Eat Dirt: Why Leaky Gut May be the Root Cause of Your Health Problems, (Bluebird, London).

Dr Norman W. Walker (1970), Fresh Vegetable and Fruit Juices, (Norwalk Press, Summertown).

Dr Norman W. Walker (1978), Become Younger, (Norwalk Press, Summertown).

Dr Norman Walker, (1979), Colon Health – Key to Vibrant Life, (Norwalk Press, Summertown).)

Gabriel Cousens (2000), Conscious Eating, (Berkeley, North Atlantic Books, California).

Joel Furham (2003), Eat to Live (New York: Little, Brown and Company).

Joshua Collins (2013) Coconut Oil Handbook: Nature's miracle for weight loss, hair loss and a beautiful you! (USA).

Markus Rothrkranz (2013), Heal Your Face, (Rothkranz Publishing).

Markus Rothkranz (2013), Heal Yourself 101, (Rothkranz Publishing).

Melissa Perlman and Erica Gragg (2007), Bikini Bootcamp, (Broadway Books, USA).

Patrick Holford (2017), Improve your Digestion, (Little, Brown Book Group, London).

Paul C. Bragg and Patricia Bragg, Apple Cider Vinegar, Miracle Health System (Health Science, Box 7, Santa Barbara, California).

Robert O. Young (2002), The pH Miracle, (New York: Wellness Central).

Tom Bohager (2002), Enzymes: What the Experts Know, (Prescott, AZ One World Press).

T. Colin Campbell (2006), The China Study, (BenBella Books).